Intellect:

Mind Over Matter

ALSO BY MORTIMER J. ADLER

Dialectic
What Man Has Made of Man
How to Read a Book
How to Think About War and Peace
The Capitalist Manifesto (with Louis O. Kelso)
The Idea of Freedom
The Conditions of Philosophy
The Difference of Man and the Difference It Makes
The Time of Our Lives
The Common Sense of Politics
The American Testament (with William Gorman)
Some Questions About Language
Philosopher at Large
Great Treasury of Western Thought (with Charles Van Doren)
Aristotle for Everybody
How to Think About God
Six Great Ideas
The Angels and Us
The Paideia Proposal
How to Speak / How to Listen
Paideia Problems and Possibilities
A Vision of the Future
The Paideia Program
Ten Philosophical Mistakes
A Guidebook to Learning
We Hold These Truths
Reforming Education (ed. by Geraldine Van Doren)

Intellect:
Mind Over Matter

MORTIMER J. ADLER

COLLIER BOOKS
Macmillan Publishing Company
New York

Maxwell Macmillan Canada
Toronto

Maxwell Macmillan International
New York   Oxford   Singapore   Sydney

Copyright © 1990 by Mortimer J. Adler

Collier Books
Macmillan Publishing Company
866 Third Avenue
New York, NY 10022

Maxwell Macmillan Canada, Inc.
1200 Eglinton Avenue East
Suite 200
Don Mills, Ontario M3C 3N1

Macmillan Publishing Company is part of the
Maxwell Communication Group of Companies.

Library of Congress Cataloging-in-Publication Data
Adler, Mortimer Jerome, 1902–
    Intellect: mind over matter / Mortimer J. Adler.—1st Collier
Books ed.
        p.   cm.
    Originally published: New York: Macmillan; London: Collier
Macmillan, c1990.
    Includes bibliographical references and index.
    ISBN 0-02-001015-X
    1. Intellect.   2. Philosophy of mind.   3. Mind and body.
I. Title.
[BF431.A44   1993]   93–1135   CIP
128′.2—dc20

Macmillan books are available at special discounts for bulk
purchases for sales promotions, premiums, fund-raising, or
educational use. For details, contact:
Special Sales Director
Macmillan Publishing Company
866 Third Avenue
New York, NY 10022

First Collier Books Edition 1993

10   9   8   7   6   5   4   3   2   1

Printed in the United States of America

CONTENTS

III
THE POWERS OF THE INTELLECT

IV
THE USE, MISUSE, AND NONUSE
OF THE INTELLECT

The Reasons for This Book

THE REASONS ARE NOT far to seek. They can be found in the title of this book.

Three words in the title go a long way toward telling the whole story—"mind," "matter," and "intellect." The contemporary view of mind denies the intellect as a distinct faculty—a special power of the human mind that makes it radically different in kind, not just in degree, from the minds of all other animals on earth.

When the intellect is ignored or denied as a distinctive faculty of the human mind, mind and matter tend to coalesce. It is almost as if the recognition of the intellect were required to preserve the separation of mind from matter, or, to go a step further, to declare the superiority of mind over matter and the irreducibility of mind to matter.

In books that dominate the contemporary literary scene, the word "mind" is used as a synonym for "body." For example, the Oxford University Press has recently published an 826-page volume entitled *The Oxford Companion to the Mind*. In a review of that book, the *London Economist* opened by saying: "For mind, read body. Much of *The*

Oxford Companion to the Mind is about physiology . . . so much is now known about the brain and the role it plays in mental life that to ignore it in a companion to the mind would be like writing a book about the weather and leaving out the clouds." And in its notice of the same book, *The New York Times* headed its review with the words "Neurology, Neurosis, and All That."

"Mind" and "brain"—are these interchangeable terms? They seem to be so regarded by those who approach the subject from the viewpoint of neurophysiology or neuropsychology. Yet a distinct meaning for the word "mind" persists in references to the various aspects of our mental life that the neurophysiologists think they can explain in terms of the action of the brain and central nervous system.

What is true of neurophysiologists is also true of computer technologists, especially those experimenting with the production of machine, or artificial, intelligence. A book recently published by Marvin Minsky, a professor at the Massachusetts Institute of Technology, bears the title *The Society of Mind,* though it is entirely about mechanical structures and processes.

The identification of minds with brains or minds with machines that imitate brains may be justified by the fact that these authors, who are thoroughgoing materialists, are offering neurological or mechanical explanations of what others in the general public regard as mental phenomena.

It is not only neurophysiologists and computer technologists who reductively identify mind and brain. We find the same materialism in a great deal of contemporary psychology, especially among those who call themselves behaviorists. Preeminent among them is Professor B. F. Skinner of Harvard University, who treats the mind as nothing more than a convenient fiction and regards the words we use to describe the mind as nothing but metaphors derived from words that refer to physical phenomena.

The New York Times, in reporting an address delivered by Professor Skinner at a recent meeting of the American Psychological Association, headlined its story with the words "B. F. Skinner Insists It's Just Matter Over Mind."

I would like to point out two things before I go any further. One is the curious and persistent fact that all these different forms of materialism cannot avoid using the word "mind" and all the other words that refer to mental phenomena. What makes mind a useful fiction? Why is it found indispensable by neurophysiologists, computer technologists, and behavioral psychologists? If the words that they use to describe mental states and activities are just metaphorical in meaning, why do the scientists resort to them instead of speaking more exactly in strictly literal (i.e., physical) terms?

The answer is that without some reference to mind, mental states, and mental activities, the scientists could not significantly assert their claim to having reduced mind to matter, or, if not that, at least to having explained all so-called mental phenomena in purely materialistic terms.

The conscious experience that everyone has, including the scientists who are trying to explain it, resists the attempt on anyone's part to do away entirely with all references to psychological as contrasted with physical phenomena. If all such references were banned as totally null and void, poets and novelists would be unable to put their pens to paper; and the rest of us would be unable to engage in conversations that involve the exchange of intimacies.

The second point to which attention must be called concerns the use of the word "materialism." That word is most frequently used in ordinary—nonphilosophical—speech to name a moral or cultural attitude, one that either overemphasizes or exclusively stresses the value of material possessions, the physical comforts and conveniences that money can buy and wealth can provide.

When moralists think there are more important or worthwhile goods to be sought in life, they use the term "material-ist" to condemn those who value nothing but the trappings of this world and the pleasures of the flesh, not to mention the enticements of the devil. But when we are talking about mind and matter, the words "materialism" and "materialist" are used in a quite different sense, not to signify a person's pursuit of material possessions but rather to indicate one's view of reality—of what does or does not really exist. The words are then used in a metaphysical, not a moral, sense.

The fundamental tenet of metaphysical materialism is that only material things exist—only physical bodies or quanta of physical energy. Nothing immaterial—nothing nonphysi-cal or incorporeal—exists, though some physical things or processes may have aspects that appear to be immaterial.

Metaphysical materialism, stated in these bold terms, has two obvious defects. The first is that it has its foundation in a negative proposition that has never been proved and never can be. In other words, it rests on the unprovable postulate or assumption that nothing immaterial does or can exist. That assumption may be true. Making it is not an error. Asserting it dogmatically as an established truth, however, not as something that may be assumed, *is* a serious error, a culpable mistake to be avoided.

The second defect of metaphysical materialism is its grudg-ing admission that some bodily states and physical processes have immaterial aspects. This admission by the materialist does not contradict his assertion that nothing immaterial exists—that is, nothing which is itself an immaterial entity exists in the way that bodies exist. Nevertheless, the materi-alist is compelled to admit that brain states and processes, which are material existences, do have what must be re-garded as immaterial aspects to which we cannot help refer-ring when we talk to one another about our conscious experiences.

Not all bodies or physical processes have immaterial aspects. These are to be found only in the realm of organic bodies or living organisms. We do not know with certitude, but we have no good reason to doubt that a snarling cat is feeling anger or that a whining puppy is feeling pain.

Now let me return once more to the title of this book, which states the thesis that this book aims to defend. If intellect were not a distinctive component of the human mind, a set of powers it uniquely possesses; if, in other words, the minds of men lacked intellects, then their minds would differ only in degree from the minds of other animals. But if human beings alone have minds that possess intellectual powers, then it is not matter over mind, as Professor Skinner and others assert, but rather mind over matter, as this book claims in opposition to all varieties of metaphysical materialism in the contemporary world.

We know what it means to say matter over mind—that only bodies exist and anything that appears to be immaterial cannot be more than an aspect of physical states and processes. But what does it mean to say mind over matter?

The immaterialism asserted here is not theological—not the assertion of God's existence as a purely spiritual being, nor that angels exist as incorporeal intellects, intellects without bodies. It is much more limited and qualified than that.

It asserts that the intellect is an immaterial component of human nature. The intellect cannot normally function without dependence on the activity of the brain, but the brain is not the physical organ of intellectual thought, as the eye together with the brain is the physical organ of vision.

In other words, of all the powers possessed by human beings, only our intellectual powers and operations are in themselves immaterial. Even though it must be admitted that all the activities of intellectual thought are so dependent on brain states and processes that they cannot occur without them, nevertheless, intellect as such is not reducible to brain, nor are its characteristic activities merely subjectively experienced aspects of brain states and processes.

It may be asked why, in stating the thesis of this book, have

I refrained from using the word "spiritual" and have been content with the negative term "immaterial"? The answer is that all of our knowledge and understanding is rooted in and ultimately derives from our sense-experience. It, therefore, always suffers the limitations imposed on it by its sources.

We cannot perceive spirits through our sense-organs. We have no sense-experience of anything spiritual. Hence, for us, the only significance we can attach to the word "spiritual" is limited to the negative meaning of "immaterial" —*not* material

In our ordinary daily speech, as well as in much of the literature that we read and understand, there is talk about man's spirit or about human spirituality. We seldom, if ever, pause to ask ourselves what we mean by this. Certainly nothing positive comes to mind. We have no perception of the human spirit or of the spirituality of man, nor do we have any conception of it derived from our sense-experience. To express with maximum precision the very limited understanding we have when we use these words, we would have to confine ourselves, as I have done above, to the negative significance of "immaterial."

If we were then asked why we attributed any spirit or spirituality to man (i.e., any immaterial component as belonging to his nature), only one answer that is rationally supportable is available to us: because we have intellectual powers that cannot be fully explained by the material, corporeal components of our physical makeup.

Why else do we refrain from speaking of the spirituality of dogs and cats, cows and chickens? Why do we not attribute a spiritual component to the makeup of any other animal organism? Again the answer is the same: they do not have intellect and so there is nothing immaterial in their natures.

If I were to give this book a subtitle, it would be: "The Battle of the Books in Psychology: Ancients vs. Moderns." I would be borrowing from Jonathan Swift the phrases "battle of the books" and "ancients vs. moderns," but unlike Swift I am focusing on just one part of that quarrel: namely, the battle in psychology.

There are two reasons, not just one, for writing this book. One is the defense of the immateriality of the intellect against the metaphysical materialism that is currently rampant in accounts of man's constitution and human behavior. The other is the desire to make available to readers a sounder psychology than the theories available since the seventeenth century.

I am not saying that the theories of the human mind in antiquity and in the Middle Ages were without blemish or error. There was metaphysical materialism in antiquity, notably in Democritus and other atomists. Atomism is not new, though it has become more sophisticated in modern times. There was also a totally untenable dualism of soul and body, or mind and body, to be found in the dialogues of Plato, notably the *Phaedo*. That, too, was revived in modern times with René Descartes and, in its train, with all the insolubilia of the mind-body problem.

In these respects, ancient thought can claim no advantage over modern. Both are faulted by the same errors. But ancient theories of human thought, human nature, and human behavior do contain psychological truths not to be found in the philosophical and scientific literature of modern times, especially since laboratory and experimental psychology has come into existence and since the social sciences have had their say about human behavior.

That is the one clear superiority of the ancients over the moderns in the battle of the books in psychology. Hence, here is the second reason for writing this book: to expound some truths in psychology known to the ancients but either denied, neglected, or not remembered in modern times. For whatever reason, they are truths not present in the current books that assail readers from all directions.

I have already pointed out some of the errors to be

corrected: the denial of the intellect as distinct from the senses and the imagination, and the denial of the intellect's immateriality. There are, in addition, other errors: the misunderstanding of the role of the will in relation to the passions or emotions, and the denial of its freedom of choice; mistakes about how the human mind, and especially its intellect, functions with respect to an entirely independent reality that it strives to know and understand, about how it produces the experience we have of that independent reality, and about how it confers on all the languages we use the meanings of their words, phrases, and sentences.

The immense diversity of human languages and of human cultures is quite consistent with the truth that the human mind is the same at all times and places, and with the truth that all linguistic and cultural diversities are superficial, the products of differences in nurturing, as compared with the underlying sameness of human nature and the human mind since the origin of the species *Homo sapiens* 45,000 years ago. These last two truths are generally denied or rejected by leading scientists and philosophers in this century.

The most important and noteworthy of the scientific books are written in a style that makes them inaccessible to the general reader. Their vocabularies abound in the technical jargon of their authors' specialized disciplines. They are academic books for the most part, written by professors for other professors, not for the general public. The contributions they make to the subject, especially their most important insights, remain obscure for the ordinary reader and need to be clarified.

What I have just said about the scientific books written in this century applies as well to philosophical books. Like every other academic discipline, philosophy, too, has become highly specialized. Its professors write their books for other professors to read, in the same way that they write articles in the learned journals of the philosophical profession. On the moot questions concerning the mind, about which there have been disputes down through the ages, contemporary philosophers also disagree and engage in controversy with one another. But the general, the nonacademic, reader needs help to disentangle the lines of argument and to discover on which side of the major issues the truth lies or is likely to be found.

I would like to mention one twentieth-century contribution to psychology that fits perfectly with an ancient and medieval truth: the truth about the unobservability of the mind itself. I am here referring to the contribution made by methodological behaviorism in its attack on the long tradition of modern introspective psychology, both British, German, and French, which dominated the teaching of psychology in American universities in the first quarter of this century. I was very careful to refer to the contribution of behavioristic, anti-introspective, psychology as *methodological, not metaphysical*. The latter is simply a revival or persistence of the materialistic error in psychology that reductively identifies mind with brain.

Finally, a word about myself as its author. I spent about thirty years in universities, teaching experimental psychology at Columbia University and philosophy at the University of Chicago, as well as conducting seminars on the great books that are central to philosophical thought.

Both before and after leaving academia, I have written a large number of philosophical books. With one exception, those written up through 1976 were still to a certain extent academic. Though my intention was to deal with difficult philosophical questions in a manner that was thoroughly accessible to the general reader, I did not learn how to do that effectively until after 1976. In addition, I must confess that until that time I still thought I could manage to write books that would be not only intelligible to the general reader, but also might win the attention and respect of my former academic colleagues—professors of philosophy in our universities.

Through painful experience, I finally came to realize that that double-barreled aim was impossible to achieve. Beginning with a book entitled *Aristotle for Everybody,* all the philosophical books I have written since 1977 have been aimed only at the general reader, with no concern whatsoever for the academic audience. I am not at all dismayed to report that my lack of interest in gaining the attention and respect of professors of philosophy has been met by an equal lack of attention on their part to the books I have written.

At the same time, I am pleased to report that those books have managed to attract an ever-widening circle of general readers who are interested in basic ideas and fundamental issues. I have succeeded in writing about difficult subjects and thorny problems in a manner intelligible to them. Though none has become a best-seller to the extent achieved by *How to Read a Book* in 1940, most of them have reached a substantial audience.

PART I

Basic Issues and

Questions

CHAPTER 1

Coming to Terms

IN DAILY SPEECH, most of us use the words "mind" and "intellect" in ways which indicate that an intellectual mind is our unique possession. Other animals may have minds, but they do not have intellects.

No one is given to saying that dogs, cats, horses, pigs, whales, dolphins, and chimpanzees lead intellectual lives. Nor do we say, as we often say of some human beings, that they are anti-intellectual, that they value their emotions more highly than their power of thought.

Other animals have intelligence in varying degrees. In a very general sense of the word "mind," they have minds of various capacities. But intellects? No, not in the least degree.

Intellect is man's highest power. In Roman law, that man alone has an intellect, and with it free will, is what makes human beings *persons* rather than *things*. The body of law that applies to persons is radically distinct from that which applies to things.

In Christian theology, intellect and free will are not only the foundation of human personality, but the possession of

3

an immaterial intellect is also the one characteristic of human beings that explains the passage in the opening chapter of Genesis in which it is said that man and man alone is made in God's image, for in the entire cosmos only God and the angels are pure spirits and man, among created material things, is the only living creature that has even a trace of spirituality.

In Christian theology, moreover, if there is any philosophical argument to support or lend some credibility to the dogma of the immortality of the human soul, it lies in the spirituality—that is, the immateriality—of the intellect.

Of all the serious misfortunes that can befall us while we are alive and not threatened by terminal illness, the most grievous is loss of mind or, more specifically, loss of our intellectual power—our power of rational thought.

The explanation individuals frequently give for their gravest mistakes, or even for criminal misconduct on their part, is, "I must have lost my mind. I would not have done that had I not temporarily lost my mind."

Other animals have minds, especially the vertebrates, and among them especially the higher mammals. But what human beings mean when they try to excuse themselves or explain their conduct by saying "I must have been out of my mind" or "I temporarily lost my mind" does not seem applicable to other animals. They do not appear to suffer from temporary insanity, at least not in the wild, though domesticated animals may sometimes throw fits, temporarily reverting to a savagery that their domestication was supposed to eliminate or diminish.

Deprivation of sight or hearing, partial paralysis of muscles, loss of limbs, even the conceptual blindness that is agnosia—all these misfortunes, however disabling, still allow us to live on the distinctly human plane. By resolute willpower and the exertion of mind over matter we can somehow manage to surmount the obstacles they present.

But deprived of our intellectual minds, we are deprived of our humanity.

The word "intellect" has clarity and precision in the vocabulary of philosophers up until the seventeenth century when Spinoza writes of the intellectual love of God as man's highest good. It even persists a little later in the language of the poets, as in Shelley's "Hymn to Intellectual Beauty." But after that it slowly passes out of philosophical and poetic speech. The word "mind" takes its place.

Essays are written about the human "understanding" (which is the English translation of the Greek word "nous," the word for intellect), but as that word is used it refers mainly to the operation of our sensitive faculties, not to the processes of our intellectual life.

In the literature of nineteenth- and twentieth-century psychology and in recent books about the philosophy of mind, the word "intellect" is rarely if ever used. "Intelligence" is the word that takes its place in books about the behavior of men and other animals, and what is thus referred to is found in varying degrees throughout the world of living creatures from the lowest to the highest.

When the word "mind" is now used in the behavioral sciences, it refers to what is operative in all forms of intelligent and learned behavior. It also always refers to the power and action of the senses, the imagination, and the memory, and almost never to a faculty that is solely a power of conceptual thought.

Although thought is attributed to the minds of animals other than man, their thinking is entirely circumscribed by what their sensitive powers can perceive, imagine, or remember, and never rises above their senses to move in spheres unreachable by sense. The nearest they come to being like humans is in their power of perceptual, not conceptual, thought.

In the life of all other animals, mind is embodied completely. Mind is found entirely imbedded in physical organs.

Mind is *in* matter. Only in man does mind rise *above* matter or *over* matter, by virtue of man's having a mind that has intellectual as well as sensitive powers, conceptual as well as perceptual thought, the power to think about what is unperceived and totally imperceptible.

In the vocabulary of common speech, there are a number of words that cluster around the word "mind." None of them is a precise synonym for it. Each has a somewhat different connotation and a different range of application.

Take "consciousness," for example. We realize that we are conscious by virtue of our having a mind, but we also realize that when we are asleep and not dreaming, we have a mind without being conscious. The notion of an unconscious mind carries with it the supposition that activity may go on in our minds even when we are unaware of it, activity that may manifest itself in subsequent behavior.

At the same time that we recognize that having a mind and being conscious are not identical, we also recognize that total deprivation of mind is tantamount to total lack of consciousness. But we may or may not have varying degrees of doubt about the correlation that exists between having a mind and being conscious.

In the realm of living organisms, how far down in the scale of their complexity do we go before we reach organisms that we regard as totally deprived of mind and consciousness? Is the whole realm of plants or vegetables mindless and unconscious? What about micro-organisms and the invertebrates? Among the invertebrates, insects manifest the most complex pattern of behavior; yet if all of it is completely determined by instinct, and if they manifest no capacity for learning and, through it, for modified behavior, we would not attribute even the slightest degree of intelligence to them.

We have just met another word in the cluster that surrounds the word "mind": "intelligence." Certainly, whatever has mind in any degree also has intelligence, but is the reverse true? If our use of the word "mind" is colored by our sense of our own mental abilities, we are likely to be hesitant about affirming the presence of mind in animals to which we attribute intelligence for the sole reason that they show some capacity for learned or modified behavior.

Having a mind, we are inclined to think, involves more than just the ability to learn. There is experimental evidence that amoeba and paramecia among micro-organisms can be caused to modify their behavior. They have no nervous systems, not even the very simple nervous apparatus possessed by insects. Is that fact alone sufficient to deny their possession of intelligence, consciousness, and mind? If so, how complex must an organism's nervous apparatus be to justify us in affirming that organism's possession of mind, intelligence, and consciousness?

Fortunately, we do not need to know the answers to these difficult questions, even supposing that they are answerable with some degree of assurance. Within the limits of our present concern with the human mind, we can proceed to use the three words we have been considering with meanings that justify us in attributing mind, consciousness, and intelligence to higher mammals other than man. That, in turn, is sufficient for the purpose of asking the question whether intellectual mind differs in kind or only in degree from the nonintellectual minds of other mammals, apes and dolphins, elephants and horses, lions and tigers, dogs and cats.

Before we turn from the consideration of these three words, one more, closely related to these three, deserves a moment's attention. It is the word "experience." Does the connotation of that word make it synonymous with "consciousness"? If there is no sense in speaking about our having experience in the absence of consciousness, then it would appear to follow that the range of experience enjoyed by an organism is coextensive with the range of things of which that organism is conscious.

We now come to two words in the vocabulary of our speech about mind that have critical significance for our comparison of human and nonhuman minds. They are "sense" and "intellect."

The word "sense" is generic. It covers a whole set of specific, sensitive powers, such as sight, hearing, smell, touch, and so on. It also covers certain other abilities we possess, which are dependent on the operation of our senses—namely, sense-perception, sensitive memory, and imagination.

Like "sense," the word "intellect" is also generic. It also covers a number of specific powers—the ability to conceive or understand, the ability to make judgments, and the ability to reason or make inferences. The exercise of these powers constitutes the range of human thought.

These two words—"sense" and "intellect"—raise a host of thorny problems. Are the sensitive and the intellectual powers radically distinct, so that it is possible to possess the first set without possessing the second, even though it is not possible for corporeal organisms to possess the second without possessing the first? To this question diametrically opposite answers have been given in the history of thought on the subject.

Earlier in that history, the two sets of powers were regarded as radically distinct. Later, beginning in the seventeenth century, and especially in this century, the sensitive powers came to be regarded as sufficient for the performance of all mental activities. Given the senses—and with them sense-perception, memory, and imagination—it was held to be possible for an organism to perform all the activities of thought, at least to some degree. The opposite view holds that without the intellectual in addition to the sensitive powers, either conceptual thought itself is impossible or what is peculiarly characteristic of human thought is impossible.

The introduction of the word "thought" requires us to spend a moment more on this last point. Like other words we have been considering, it has a kind of systematic ambiguity. If that were not so, we could not attribute thought to other animals as well as to human beings and we could not speak of thinking machines.

Cautioned about the ambiguity of the word "thought," we must not let the fact that we attribute thought to other animals as well as to machines lead us to the conclusion that they and we possess exactly the same powers. Animal thought and machine thought are sufficiently unlike human thought that it is necessary to attribute certain powers to the human mind not possessed by other animals or by machines.

Only if that is the case are we led to the conclusion that the human mind involves both sensitive and intellectual powers and that a distinctive intellect confers upon human beings powers not possessed by other animals or by machines.

So far we have considered words that, while not synonyms for the word "mind," have closely associated connotations. Now let us turn to words that are more like antonyms. We use the word "matter" in sharp contrast to "mind," and the word "physical" in sharp contrast to "mental." This common usage suggests that mind and matter, the mental and the physical, constitute two distinct realms, the one irreducible to the other.

This view, which in its extreme form affirms an unbridgeable gulf between the two realms, was stoutly defended in antiquity, the Middle Ages, and in early modern times. The opposite view, which in its extreme form asserts that mind and brain are identical and that the mental can be reduced to the physical, has much more currency in later centuries and especially in the present one. In between the two extremes, as we shall see, there are more moderate positions.

Since we will deal in detail with this problem later, the only point to be made here is that the resolution of this issue concerning mind and matter, the mental and the physical, is closely connected with the resolution of the issue about the difference between human minds and the minds of other animals and of machines.

The consideration of mind in relation to matter calls up two more words for consideration in this preliminary clarification of terms and issues. One is the word "soul," the other the word "spirit."

In antiquity, the word "soul" (in Greek, *psyche;* in Latin, *anima*) was used to signify whatever it was in living organisms that made them alive, active without being acted upon. Since plants are living organisms, they, too, have souls, conferring on them the vegetative powers of nourishment, growth, and reproduction. Animals have souls that confer upon them additional powers—the powers of sense, of appetite or desire, and of locomotion. In addition to endowing man with all the vital powers possessed by plants and other animals, the human soul gives man his distinctive power—that of the intellect and, with it, the power of conceptual thought, the power of judging and reasoning, and the power of making free choices.

As we have just seen, the word "soul" and the word "mind" are not coextensive in their connotations. According to the ancient doctrine being considered, all living organisms have souls, but not all have minds—vegetables, for example.

In the Christian era, theologians tended to restrict the use of the word "soul" to humans. Rejecting the doctrine of reincarnation and the transmigration of souls as heretical, Christian thinkers were concerned with the immortality of the human soul. Christian philosophers in early modern times followed suit. For them, having an intellectual or rational mind was identical with having a soul that could, as a matter of either faith or reason, be deemed immortal, which meant regarding it as capable of existing apart from the perishable body.

What does the introduction of the word "spirit" add? As I have already pointed out, it is impossible for us to say what a spirit is except in negative terms. It is the very antithesis of matter. The spiritual is the immaterial.

Plants may have souls but there is nothing spiritual about them if they are simply living bodies. The same can be said of animals, and it can also be said of human beings if the human soul differs only in degree from the souls of plants and other animals. However, when it is held that there is something spiritual about man that is not present in other living organisms, some measure of immateriality must be found in man, and it is usually found in his possession of intellect and free will.

In modern times, and especially in this century, the line that divides persons (with intellects and free will) from things has been obliterated by a predominant number of scientists and philosophers. With its removal also goes the elimination of any claim for the presence of spirituality in human nature, and in consequence the word "soul" also drops out of use. If any consideration of immateriality remains, it remains in whatever solution of the problem of the mind's relation to the body that does not go to the extreme of completely identifying the mind with the brain, thus reducing the mental to the physical.

The antithesis between bodies and minds, souls, or spirits raises the question of what is observable and what is not. If we use the word "observe" to mean that which we can perceive through the use of our senses, then minds, souls, and spirits are not observable, nor are mental powers and acts.

With regard to other organisms, whether they are brute animals or human individuals, I can observe that they have sense-organs, for these are bodily parts susceptible to sense-perception on my part; if I were a brain surgeon, I could also observe that they had brains. But still using the word "observe" for what is within the range of unaided sense-perception, I cannot observe the operations of their sense-organs, their brains, and their spinal columns. Microscopic lenses are required for that. Even with microscopes, other minds and their mental activities are not perceptually observable by us. But, you may say, that leaves one other possibility to consider. Cannot each of us observe his or her own mind and its acts?

To answer this question, it is first of all necessary to use the word "observe" in some sense other than by means of sense-perception. It is also necessary to distinguish four or five possible objects of observation. The mind itself is one of those possible objects; another is its powers; still another is whatever habits the mind forms; and, finally, we have mental acts themselves and the mental products of those acts, such as perceptions, memories, images, and thoughts.

The special kind of observation that is thought to occur when individuals are supposed to be able to observe the objects mentioned above has been called introspection. All five of those objects are certainly objects of thought on my part; otherwise I could not be considering them at all. But three of them are just as certainly not objects capable of being observed introspectively—the mind itself, its powers, and its habits. What I have to say about them is a result of inference on my part, not introspective observation.

Two objects remain: the various acts of the mind, and the products of these acts. I can say, as a matter of my own experience (as you probably can, too), that I am reflexively aware of the actions of my mind when and as I perform them. I am aware that I am perceiving when I perceive; of remembering when I remember; of imagining when I imagine; and of thinking when I think. This much, at least, would appear to fall within the bounds of introspective observation.

But, as I will explain at length later, what is beyond my introspective observation are the products of these activities, products that are sometimes referred to as the contents of the mind. With one exception that I will mention later, the contents of my mind are totally beyond observation, certainly by you and even by me trying to observe introspectively.

The reason I broach this point before I can enter into a satisfactory discussion of it is in order to point out the only method available to us in all our dealings with the human mind. Apart from the reflexive awareness that each of us has of his or her own mind's activity, all the rest, with the one exception mentioned above, comes to us by inference. With regard to the minds of other human beings, we do not have even reflexive awareness. We only have what can be culled by inference from our observation through sense-perception of their bodily behavior and from our interpretation of their speech. In the case of brute animals, we do not have even speech as a basis for inference about their minds, or their mental powers and acts.

In the next chapter, I will try to explain at length why, like the behaviorists of this century, beginning with John B. Watson, I reject the whole tradition of introspective psychology that had its beginnings in early modern times with Thomas Hobbes and John Locke.

In chapter 3, I will try to defend the uniqueness of the human mind by virtue of its having an intellect and thus being different in kind from the minds of other animals. In chapter 4, I will explain the immateriality of the intellect and argue against its nonidentity with the brain. In chapter 5, I will give reasons for thinking it improbable that intelligent machines will ever be constructed with the power to do everything that an intellect can do. In chapter 6, I will consider the possibility of intelligent creatures elsewhere in the universe and, if they exist, what kind of minds they might have.

The questions that we will confront in the set of chapters that follow in Part II are of a different order: in chapter 8, the question about the mind's relation to reality; in chapter 9, the question about the relation of our experience of reality to reality itself; in chapter 10, the question about the influence of language upon the operations of our minds; and in chapter 11, the question whether cultural differences are due solely to differences in the way the human mind is nurtured.

I would like to close these preliminary clarifications with one comment on the chapters of Part I as outlined above. Here the views I shall be expressing and the positions on disputed issues that I shall be defending may or may not strike ordinary readers as being in agreement with the commonsense views they themselves hold as a result of their common experience.

However, in Part II, beginning with chapter 7 on philosophy and common sense, I will try to show that the views I am expressing are, I think, the views held by most of my readers as their commonsense convictions in the light of common human experience. It is here that I will be most at pains to argue for the commonsense view that all human beings live in one and the same world, that our experience of that world's reality is the same in its character and operations as are the minds of every human being alive now or in the past and future.

CHAPTER 2

Is the Mind Observable?

AT THE BEGINNING of this century an American psychologist, Professor John B. Watson of Johns Hopkins University, wrote a book entitled *Psychology from the Standpoint of a Behaviorist*. When I was a junior instructor in psychology at Columbia University in the early 1920s, I used Watson's book in the elementary psychology classes that I taught.

The doctrine was extremely simple, almost simplistic. We come into this world with a relatively small number of innate reflexes, some congenital, some not. These are, of course, directly observable in the behavior of the infant. All further behavioral developments result from the conditioning of these reflexes, and those conditioned reflexes are also directly observable. When it expresses itself in overt, verbal behavior, even thought is observable, but it still remains a series of muscular acts of subvocal speech when the thinking that goes on is inaudible.

The basic terms of behavioristic psychology were stimulus and response—both observable entities. Behaviorism departed from its methodological rule of confining itself to the observable when it allowed itself to infer the existence of mediating nervous centers that connect stimuli with responses. That one inference did not alter its insistence upon observing the behavior elicited by the applied stimuli.

From the standpoint of the behaviorist and his stimulus-response approach, no difference existed between the laboratory study of human and animal behavior. In sharp contrast, the older introspective psychology that behaviorism sought to replace was necessarily a study of the human, not the animal, mind.

If psychology were ever to become a science comparable to other natural sciences, Watson contended, it would have to proceed by restricting itself to perceivable phenomena— phenomena that were public in the sense that they were open to observation by any number of independent observers. That, of course, ruled out introspective observation of the mind's acts and contents by any one individual in a position to make such observations.

Watson went further and denied that there was a mind (as distinct from the brain and central nervous system) in which there existed anything observable, even introspectively. At that point he went beyond being a behaviorist for the sake of scientific method in psychology. Like Professor Skinner later, Professor Watson took sides on a philosophical issue, aligning himself with materialists who denied the existence of anything except bodies, and therefore, he reductively identified minds with brains.

Watson was both right and wrong. He was right in thinking that if minds did exist in any way that was distinct from brains, they, unlike bodies, were intrinsically unobservable by the senses. Only bodies and their motions are thus observable. But he was wrong in concluding that because minds are not observable in the way that bodies are they therefore do not exist. That piece of reasoning is the classic non sequitur of materialism.

What Watson failed to realize is that the existence of the unobservable can be affirmed as a result of inferences made from observed phenomena. Far from being a departure from scientific method, making such inferences, when necessary, is acceptable procedure.

In dismissing introspective observation as entirely chimerical, Watson also went too far. He was right in maintaining that thoughts themselves cannot be observed but wrong in denying that thinking persons are not aware that they are thinking when that activity is occurring in their minds. You and I and everyone else are directly acquainted with the acts of our own minds. We know the difference between thinking and remembering, between remembering and imagining, between imagining and perceiving, between perceiving and desiring, between desiring and feeling or emotion.

One of the special properties of the human mind is its reflexive awareness of its own acts and, through that, its ability to distinguish the mind's different activities from one another. To this extent, and only to this extent, is the mental as well as the physical observable, the one introspectively, the other by sense-perception.

I said a moment ago that though Watson went too far in dismissing introspective observation as entirely chimerical, he was correct in denying that the contents of the mind— the products of its acts—are open to inspection by the mind itself. We can be aware that we are thinking, or imagining, or perceiving, but we cannot, by looking inside our minds, find any thoughts or concepts, any images or any perceptions there.

To say that we cannot observe them by introspection is not to say that they do not exist. Rather, it is to say that they are there and that they function in a self-effacing manner to present to the mind the objects that we experience when we are conscious, objects that are public in the sense that others either do or can experience them, too.

Let me stress that if the contents of my mind (its thoughts or concepts, memories, images, perception, or desires) were introspectively observable objects, *as they are not,* they would be private, not public, objects, observable by me and by me alone.

One exception to this statement must be added at once. Certain bodily feelings that I have had, such as a toothache or the soreness of a muscle, are experiences for me alone. They are purely subjective experiences to which I alone have privileged access. You, too, have such purely subjective experiences that cannot be objects of my awareness.

In sharp contrast to such uniquely subjective experiences, whatever is for me an experienced object is or can be an experienced object for you also. Therein lies the meaning of the word "objective," signifying what either is or can be the same for two or more individuals.

I have already acknowledged that the view I have just expressed concerning the unobservability—even by introspection—of the mind's contents (with the one exception noted) is a view not held by people in general. It is my impression that most people today make the same mistake that was made for centuries by introspective psychologists who supposed they could look into the mind and explore or examine its contents.

That mistake had its origin at the beginning of modern philosophy when such thinkers as René Descartes in France and John Locke in England regarded the ideas in each person's mind as its primary objects—in fact, the only objects with which that person had direct acquaintance. In expounding this view, they used the word "idea" to stand for all the diverse contents of the mind, the products of all its acts.

I have no difficulty in explaining how these philosophers made that mistake.* But I find it difficult to explain how so

---

*In the first chapter of *Ten Philosophical Mistakes* (1985), I accounted for the origin of the error by calling attention to a distinction made earlier in philosophical thought that Descartes and Locke either missed or ignored. That distinction is between ideas as that by which *(id quo)* the mind apprehends the objects of thought, and those objects as that which *(id quod)* are thereby apprehended.

mistaken a view could have become generally prevalent among ordinary folk. It is, of course, possible that the mistake filtered down or flowed over from academic circles to the public generally, but that seems unlikely. A more reasonable explanation is that the wrong view is simply easier for anyone, including philosophers, to grasp. The correct view of the matter does involve some refinements and subtleties that require one to use language with greater precision than usual.

Let us consider your having a toothache at this moment, which you can tell me about but which I cannot experience at the same time, though I understand what you are telling me because, I, too have had a toothache in the past. Let us also consider us to be engaged in conversation about a painting on the wall of the room in which we are both sitting. We are talking about one and the same painting, which is a visual object that we are both looking at. We are not talking about our individually different acts of looking at the painting, nor are we talking about the visual percept in your mind and the visual percept in my mind, which are produced by the act of vision when each of us looks at the painting on the wall.

In the case of the toothache, the subject of our conversation is just one thing: your subjective and private feeling, with which I have some sympathy as a result of my having had similar feelings. In the case of the painting, the subject of our conversation is also just one thing: the visual object that we are both looking at. But in the case of the painting, other factors are involved in our being able to have that one object before us as *that which* we are talking about.

The two words "that which" give us the clue to what else is involved. Your visual percept and my visual percept, the one in my mind produced by my act of perceiving, the other in your mind produced by your act of perceiving, are *that by which* we are able to have the same visual object before us for discussion. When your toothache is *that which* we are talking about, what enables us to talk about it is, on your part, the feeling you are directly experiencing and, on my part, my memory of having had a similar feeling. When the painting on the wall is the object of our conversation (*that which* we are talking about), what enables us to do so (*that by which* we are able to do so) are the perceptions each of us has as the result of our acts of perceiving it.

If my perception of the painting and your perception of the painting were the objects of our *separate* minds (*that which* each of us introspectively observed), then we would not and could not be talking about the painting on the wall. Only if the perception in your mind and the perception in my mind are *that by which* we are aware or conscious of the painting on the wall can that be a common or public object which we are able to discuss.

This removes the puzzle about how we can know that our minds do have contents (such as perceptions, memories, or thoughts), which are the products of our mental activities (such as perceiving, remembering, and thinking), even though we cannot introspectively discover the existence of such mental products by looking into our minds and becoming aware of their presence there. The solution of the puzzle is an inference on our part, an inference we cannot avoid making if we acknowledge that effects must have causes.

That which we have before our minds as an object (the painting on the wall) presupposes *that by which* one and the same object exists for both of us (the perception of it in my mind and the perception of it in yours). Each of us is directly aware of his own act of perceiving. And even though we are not directly aware of the perception that that act produces, we infer that it exists as a result of the act of perceiving because it is for each of us *that by which* we have the same object before us as a subject for discussion.

If the supposed introspectively observed contents of the mind—its percepts, memories, images, and thoughts, concepts, or ideas—called attention to themselves, they would necessarily distract our attention from the objects that we consciously experience. If they drew attention to themselves exclusively, such attention would exclude those objects entirely from our conscious experience.

The objects we consciously experience are of two sorts: private and public. Private are all bodily feelings and emotions—feelings of pleasure and pain, of hunger and thirst, of fear and anger. These private objects of consciousness belong exclusively in the experience of this individual or that. Public are the objects that we and others apprehend in common, and being the same objects experienced by two or more individuals can be talked about by them.

This distinction between public and private objects of our conscious experience calls for a parallel distinction between two kinds of mental processes: cognitive and affective. The affects are directly experienced bodily feelings and emotions. They are always *that which* we experience, never *that by which* we experience something. In sharp contrast, cognitions—perceptions, memories, imaginations, and thoughts—are always *that by which* we experience the objects they make present to our minds. They are *never* the experienced objects themselves, never *that which* is apprehended by the mind.

In denying an introspective awareness of the cognitive contents of the mind, I would describe myself as a methodological behaviorist. I agree with Professor John B. Watson that, apart from subjectively experienced bodily feelings, the contents of the mind cannot be introspectively observed. At the same time, I disagree with his metaphysical materialism—his assertion that only bodies and their motions exist and his denial that anything mental exists.

To be a methodological, but not materialistic, behaviorist is to take the position that whatever can be said about the mind and its contents, or its processes and products, neither of which can be directly observed, must be inferred from behavior that is directly observed. From the observable fact that you and I are discussing a painting on the wall, I need not infer that each of us is perceiving it, for that is an act of our minds that each of us can introspectively observe. But I must infer that there is in my mind a percept and in your mind a percept—products of our acts of perceiving, *that by which* the painting has become an object we can discuss with one another.

That is the first inference I must make as a methodological behaviorist. A second inference is that each of us, being reflexively aware of the acts of his or her own mind, can infer that minds have certain generic powers, and also as many different specific powers as there are distinct types of mental acts that we are able to perform. On what basis do we distinguish the diverse powers of our mind or the diverse acts that are the basis for inferring the existence of these powers?

The answer, given briefly here and explained more fully in chapter 12, is that the acts of the mind are differentiated from one another as different types of mental activity and by differences in their objects. It follows, of course, that different types of mental activity presuppose generically different types of mental power.

Let us assume for the moment a point that will be defended later: that the human mind is the same mind in all human beings. This means that each of us has the same set of mental powers. Yet though we all have the same powers, we do not all behave in the same way. From those behavioral differences we infer that some of us perform mental acts not performed by others.

Why not, since all of us have the same mental powers? That being so, why do we not all perform the same mental acts? The answer must be that the mental powers some of us possess were developed by nurturing of a certain sort. Through such nurturing, we have formed habits not possessed by those who lacked that nurturing.

Are those habits of mind directly observable? No, they are not observable by those who possess them. But their existence can be inferred from what is distinctive about the observable behavior of the persons who have such habits.

Finally, we come to the mind itself. It certainly is not observable as bodies are. But if all the foregoing inferences from observable behavior are justified, and if they are taken together with the reflexive awareness that each of us has of his or her own mental activity, then we should have no difficulty in inferring the existence of the mind—the seat of mental powers, the performer of mental acts.

At this point we encounter a paradox. The materialists who deny the existence of anything that is not a body, and, therefore, reductively identify the mind with the brain, must hold the view that, insofar as the mind is identical with the brain, it is just as observable as any body or bodily organ. But if that is the case, why use the word "mind" at all?

Either the word "mind" has some meaning that is distinct from the meaning of the word "brain," in which case mind is *not* observable, *or* "mind" and "mental activity" refer to nothing that is distinct from the brain and its processes, in which case mind *is* observable.

Points that have been covered in this chapter obviously have a bearing on the issue we will come to in chapter 4. I should go further and add that what has been said here precludes an acceptance of the extreme form of the identity hypothesis, which completely reduces mind to brain.

CHAPTER 3

Is Our Intellect Unique?

I HAVE ASSERTED that intellectual mind is exclusively human. Is that true? Do human beings differ from other animals in kind or only in degree? And if in kind, is man's possession of an intellect the basis for that difference in kind?

These two questions are inseparable. How we answer one determines our answer to the other. In a book I wrote some years ago, *The Difference of Man and the Difference It Makes* (1967), I had compelling reasons for concluding that man differed radically in kind from other animals, including those to which the human species is genealogically most closely related. Reviewing evidence that has come forward in the last twenty years, I have stronger reasons now for defending the same conclusion.

Man's difference in kind rests largely on the uniqueness of the human intellect as that manifests itself in behavior that is peculiarly human. There are certainly other anatomical and physiological differences between the human and other mammalian species. These may be either differences in kind or in degree. If they are differences in kind, they may be related to the behavioral differences with which we are immediately concerned.

Before I come to what makes the intellect unique and the basis for a radical difference in kind between man and other animals, let me spend a moment on the distinction between difference in degree and difference in kind, and on what makes a difference in kind radical rather than superficial.

Two things differ in degree when, with respect to a certain property that they have in common, one has more of it and the other less. In geometry, two triangles differ in degree with respect to their area if one is larger and the other smaller. In the physical world, two runways on an airfield differ in degree if one is longer, the other shorter.

Two things differ in kind when one of them has characteristics or properties not possessed by the other. In geometry, a triangle and a circle differ in kind by virtue of the fact that one figure has angles and the other has none. In the physical world, invertebrates and vertebrates differ in kind. The latter have backbones lacked by the former.

A single property present in one thing and absent in another is sufficient to differentiate two things in kind. Additional respects that differentiate two things in kind by their presence in the one and their absence in the other do not increase the difference in kind. They merely give us greater assurance that we are correct in regarding the two things as different in kind.

That is the way things stand in the case of man in relation to other animals. Our assurance about that difference in kind arises from the substantial number of respects in which we find human beings behaving in ways that are totally missing from the behavior of other animals. In these respects we find nothing similar there, even in the slightest degree.

This is not to say that there are no similarities between human and animal behavior, just as there are many anatomical and physiological similarities between human and mammalian bodies. Differences in kind do not preclude differences in degree. Pointing out the many respects in which humans and other animals differ only in the degree to which they possess the same traits or manifest the same behavior does not constitute an argument against their also being different in kind.

One distinction remains to be considered, and it is of the greatest importance here: that is the distinction between a difference in kind that is radical and one that is superficial.

I attach the word "superficial" to a difference in kind if it exists on the surface but exists there only because of an underlying difference in degree. In other words, the difference in kind under observation is superficial if it can be attributed to a difference in degree that is its cause.

Three states of matter—solid, liquid, and gaseous—appear to differ in kind. We can walk on water that is frozen solid, swim in liquid water, and inhale the gaseous vapors that arise from boiling water. The chemical constitution of the matter is the same in all three cases. The three different states of the same kind of matter result from differences of degree with regard to the character and velocity of molecular motion in the solid, liquid, and gaseous states. Hence, while the three states differ in kind, that difference in kind is superficial, not radical.

You and I would feel more comfortable if I could give you an example of a radical difference in kind drawn from the physical world or even from the world of living organisms. I hesitate to do so because with regard to any instance that I can think of in the realm of inorganic bodies or in the domain of living organisms below the level of man, I am relatively confident that someone would be able to show an underlying difference in degree in my example's physical constitution of the things that only makes it appear to be different in kind.

The reason why this may be disturbing to you and me is that a radical difference in kind between man and other animals, if it exists, would be the one and only breach in the continuity of nature. That would be a remarkable singularity, calling for an explanation that might or might not be forthcoming or satisfactory.

By analogy with the superficial difference in kind between the solid, liquid, and gaseous states of matter, it is possible that many differences in kind between the behavior of human beings and other animals arises solely from a difference in degree between the size and complexity of the human brain and central nervous system and that of other animals. Were that the case, were the behavioral differences in kind completely explained by underlying neurological differences in degree, then the difference in kind would be superficial, not radical.

To say "completely explained" may be going too far, in view of the fact that there appear to be certain anatomical differences in kind between the human brain and nervous apparatus and that of man's closest biological relatives, the anthropoid apes. In the human brain, there is an area, Broca's motor center for speech, not found in other animals. The functional asymmetry of the two hemispheres of the human cerebral context is also uniquely human.

Do these two anatomical differences enter into the explanation of the behavioral differences in kind? Do they make that difference in kind radical rather than superficial, in spite of the fact that it may also be an effect of differences in degree between the nervous apparatus in man and in other animals? I am not prepared to answer this question, but it should be kept in mind as we turn now to another approach to the radical character of the difference in kind between man and other animals.

That difference would be radical if it arose from something in the human constitution that is not present in the constitution of comparable species. Brains and other nervous apparatus are present in both, differing in degree certainly and perhaps also in kind. But if the human mind is unique as compared with the minds of all other animals, and if its uniqueness is the cause of the manifest difference in kind between human behavior and the behavior of other animals, then we are justified in regarding that difference in kind as radical rather than superficial. It is difference rooted in a property of human nature not present in any other species.

We can be clear about the respects in which the human mind is not unique. Like us, other animals have sensory organs that together with their brains function in acts of sense-perception. I would go further and say that, in light of evidence drawn from elaborate experimentation with animals, perceptual thought can also be attributed to them—abstraction of a certain sort and also generalization. They may have, in rudimentary degrees, memory and imagination. Without any doubt, they as well as we have appetitive impulses, desires that motivate and drive them into action, and they certainly have emotions that we, too, share—anger and fear.

With regard to most of the similarities just mentioned, human beings and other animals differ in degree. But there are two exceptions and these go to the heart of the matter. They give us the clue to the human mind's uniqueness, which consists in its having intellectual powers not possessed by the minds of other animals.

While thought is present in both man and the higher animals, animal thought is perceptual thought; only human thought is conceptual. While motivating appetites or desires are present in both man and other animals, only man has an intellectual appetite, a will that is able to make free choices.

I have just made a series of assertions that I am prepared to and will presently defend. But before I do I must add that man's possession of intellectual powers, which are not present in other animals, does not suffice to make man's difference in kind radical. It might still be superficial if the operation of those intellectual powers can be adequately explained neurologically in a way that ultimately involves differences in degree between man and other animals.

This means that the questions raised at the opening of this chapter cannot be fully answered here. What remains to be done, then, serves as preparation for the arguments to come. Let me enumerate, first of all, those things that are distinctive about human behavior.

Other animals live entirely in the present. Only human individuals are time-binders, connecting the perceived present with the remembered past and the imaginable future. Only man is a historical animal with a historical tradition and a historical development. In the case of other species, the life of succeeding generations remains the same as long as no genetic changes occur. Human life, however, changes from one generation to another with the transmission of cultural novelties and with accretion of accumulated cultural changes and institutional innovations. Nothing like these innovations and changes can be found in any other species.

Other animals make things, such as hives, nests, dams, and, in the case of birds, songs. It may even be that in doing so, other animals use rudimentary tools as well as their own appendages. But only man makes machines, which are not hand tools, for the purpose of making products that cannot be produced in any other way.

It is not enough to say that man is the only manufacturing animal. We must add that he is the only machinofacturing animal. The kind of thought that is involved in designing and building a machine betokens the presence of an intellect in a way that the use of hand tools does not.

Among the things that man makes are works of art that we regard as fine rather than useful, because they are made for the pleasure or enjoyment they afford rather than to serve some further purpose. Are the songs made by birds comparable?

No, because even if the songs birds make serve no biological purpose and are simply made to be enjoyed, the songs made by a given species of bird remain the same for all members of that species generation after generation.

In contrast, in the making of drawings or paintings, from the sketches drawn on the walls of the Cro-Magnon caves down to the present day, the extraordinary variety in human works of art shows that human artistry is not instinctive, and therefore not the same for all members of the species from one generation to the other. To say that human artistry is creative, not instinctive, is to say that it consists of acts voluntarily done, involving both thought and choice on the part of the individual artist.

The comparison of man as a social animal with other social animals runs parallel to the comparison just made between man's artistry and animal productivity. The other social animals are instinctively gregarious, not voluntarily or inventively so. Being instinctive, the pattern of their social behavior remains the same from generation to generation and wherever we find individuals that are members of the species.

Human societies are extraordinarily various, though the members of them are all individuals of the same species. They are governed by rules or laws and customs that are handed down from generation to generation as well as altered from time to time. Passing beyond family and tribal groups, which are immensely diverse in their organization and customs, and coming to the larger and more inclusive association that we call a state, we are justified in regarding man as the only *political* animal—the only animal that, either by the voluntary establishment of a constitution or by entering voluntarily into a social contract, brings the state, the political community or civil society, into existence.

As I see it, all the differences in kind so far mentioned cannot be explained except by reference to man's exclusive possession of an intellect, with its power of conceptual thought and with the power of free choice. When we consider man's syntactical speech and the variety of human languages, and compare them with such use of symbols as human experimenters have managed to confer upon chimpanzees, we reach the same conclusion. The difference is one of kind and it can be explained only by the uniqueness of the human mind because of its intellectual powers—conceptual thought and free choice.

The observable behavioral differences between human and other animals to which I have called attention cannot be denied, but the fact that they must be acknowledged does not settle the matter. Those who, since Darwin's day, are more and more insistent that only a difference in degree prevails try to explain away the observed facts.

The two things to which they appeal in order to do so are (1) the experimental evidence of what they regard as linguistic behavior on the part of chimpanzees, admittedly vastly different in degree from human speech; and (2) laboratory findings with regard to thinking and problem-solving on the part of animals much lower in the scale than apes. It is necessary, therefore, for me to point out why these efforts fail to change the picture.

1. *With regard to the linguistic behavior of chimpanzees.* In the first place, such linguistic behavior as has been observed occurs under laboratory conditions, not in the wild. There is much evidence that animals in the wild do communicate with one another by cries or sounds of various sorts and by bodily gestures, including facial grimaces. But all these animal expressions function as signals, communicating emotional states, desires, or purposes. None is a designative

sign functioning, as a word does in human language, to name something.

However, this is precisely what those who have worked with chimpanzees claim behavioral scientists are able to do: namely, teach (or perhaps a better word would be "train") the chimpanzees to use symbols in a designative fashion to name things. They appear to have succeeded in doing this, at least to the extent of the chimp's acquiring several hundred different symbols.

The symbols, it should be noted at once, are not like words in human language, for they are not related to one another as different parts of speech. It should also be noted that no older chimpanzee, having acquired a rudimentary vocabulary of the sort indicated, ever transmits that vocabulary to a younger chimpanzee. In other words, whereas in the human world a language is transmitted from one generation to another, nothing like that occurs in the world of the chimpanzee.

In the third place, the set of symbols that appears to function for chimpanzees as name-words function in human language are strictly limited to the designation of perceptible objects that are also actually perceived. None ever designates a perceptible object that has not been actually perceived by the animal. None ever designates a totally imperceptible object. In sharp contrast, human language contains a vast number of words that function designatively in both these ways: not only to name objects that, though perceptible, have not been perceived, but also to name objects that are imperceptible.

This last point brings us, finally, to the most critical difference between humans and chimpanzees with regard to linguistic behavior. Let us compare scientists training chimpanzees in the use of symbols and parents teaching their children the use of words. In the latter case, the learning process takes two forms. Children learn the meaning of a word by having it repeatedly applied to an object that is perceptually present—the dog in front of them, the spoon in their hands. But children can acquire significant words in a quite different way, not by direct perceptual acquaintance with the object named, but by a verbal description of the object designated.

For example, a child hears the word "kindergarten" for the first time and asks what it means. When told that a kindergarten is a place where children play with one another and also learn, the word "kindergarten" has acquired sufficient meaning for that child to be used significantly before he or she ever goes to kindergarten.

Although the first words that children learn to use significantly are all words the meanings of which have been learned by perceptual acquaintance with the objects named, somewhat later in the growth of the child's vocabulary, a much larger number of new words become meaningful in the other way—by verbal description of objects signified rather than by direct perceptual acquaintance with them. This second way of acquiring meaningful designations has never occurred in the linguistic training of chimpanzees. Though "never" is a daring word to use about the future, I dare to say it never will.

Why do we find these differences between the linguistic training of chimpanzees and the learning of a language by human beings? Because the mind of the chimpanzee, like the minds of all other animals, consists solely of sensory powers and so cannot rise above the level of sense-perception, whereas the human mind has intellectual as well as sensory powers and can operate on the level of conceptual thought as well as on the level of sense-perception. Far from providing evidence against the uniqueness of the human mind, all the experimental work that has been done with the use of symbols by chimpanzees confirms it.

2. *With regard to thinking and problem-solving by animals.* A vast amount of experimental work has been done on animal learning. I will confine myself here to laboratory experiments in which animals learn to discriminate between one type of object and another, and to rise above particulars, achieving what looks like generalizations. In these experiments, animals react to a particular stimulus in a particular way, then transfer that response to other stimuli that are like it in type, though not like it in all respects. For example, animals finding their food placed on square mats rather than round ones will later go to square mats for their food even if the squares are larger or smaller than the original ones and are of a different color.

The amount of variation in the set of stimuli that can still elicit the same response measures the degree of similarity required in order for the differing stimuli to function as equivalent. Some, though not all, of the psychologists who have performed such experiments infer that because animals can discriminate between different types of objects, they are engaged in concept-formation and have some ability to generalize from their experiences. If that conclusion were justified by the experimental evidence, it would undermine the view that concept-formation and generalization require intellectual powers that are uniquely human.

It has been pointed out by an eminent neurologist, Professor K. S. Lashley, that when human beings recognize the letter A, even though it appears to them in a wide variety of visible shapes, they show themselves capable of perceptual abstraction. But when they are able to recognize that an English and a German sentence have the same meaning, they rise above the perceptual level, for what is grasped by the human mind here is something common to the two sentences even though they have no sensible resemblance to one another.

Another commentator on the laboratory evidence, this time a philosopher, Peter Geach, writes:

Many psychologists, wishing to use the word "concept" far more widely than I do . . . would say that an animal has acquired a concept if it has learned a discriminative response to some feature of its environment. If a rat or dog is trained to react in a certain way whenever it has a triangle shown to it (rather than some other shape), then they would say it has acquired the concept of triangle. . . . What is at issue here is not just the way the term "concept" is used, but the desirability of comparing these achievements of rats and dogs with the performances of human beings who possess a concept of *triangle*. . . . The life of brutes lacks so much that is integral to human life that it can only be misleading to say that they have concepts like us—as misleading as it would be to say that men have tails and that women lay eggs. . . . Experience in training dogs to "recognize" triangles can be no guide in (let us say) teaching geometry.

At the risk of belaboring this point unduly, I wish to take a moment to be as precise as possible about the difference between perceptual and conceptual thought.

Two things must be said about concepts. The first is that concepts are (a) acquired dispositions to recognize perceived objects as being of this or that kind and at the same time (b) to understand what this kind or that kind of object is like, with the result (c) that the individual having formed a concept is able to perceive a number of sensible particulars as being of the same kind and to discriminate between them and other sensible particulars that are different in kind.

The second thing that must be said about concepts is that they are acquired dispositions to understand what certain types of objects are like, both when they are not actually perceived and also when they are not perceptible.

What the experimental work done on animal discrimination shows is that animals acquire dispositions to perceive a number of sensible particulars as being of the same kind and to distinguish between them and other perceived particulars that are different in kind. Such acts of perceptual abstraction by animals coincide with just one of the many aspects of concept-formation. Concept-formation by human beings enables them to perceive a number of sensible particulars as being of the same kind and to discriminate between them and other sensible particulars that are different in kind. In this respect, it does for human beings what perceptual abstraction does for other animals.

But perceptual abstraction does not enable animals to do any of the other things that concept-formation enables human beings to do. It does not provide an understanding of certain types of objects both when they are not actually perceived and also when they are imperceptible, nor does it provide any understanding of what this or that kind of object is like quite apart from the perception of it.*

The experimentally observed behavior of animals can be adequately explained in terms of perceptual abstractions and by reference to processes of perceptual generalization and discrimination that give rise to perceptual abstractions. Concepts (understood as quite distinct from perceptual abstractions) and concept-formation (understood as quite distinct from perceptual generalization and discrimination) are not needed to explain the observed behavior of animals.

I cannot resist digressing for a moment to comment on a peculiarly human neurological malady known as agnosia. A wonderfully interesting account of it has been written by Dr. Oliver Sacks in his book, *The Man Who Mistook His Wife for a Hat.*

Agnosia occurs in individuals whose sensory powers are in no way impaired but who have suddenly become concep-

---

*We know something that is true of all perceptible and imaginable triangles, triangles of every shape and size: namely, that all are three-sided figures with three angles between which no diagonals can be drawn. The object so defined is an intelligible object of thought and gives general significance to the word "triangle."

tually, not perceptually, blind. Dr. Sacks's patient, who mistook his wife for a hat, could give a good verbal description of the visible appearance of a certain object, but he could not tell that it was a glove until he touched it and put it on. He could vividly describe the visible appearance of a rose, but he could not recognize it as a rose until he smelled it.

His conceptual blindness occurred only in the field of vision, not in that of any other sense. I shall return to the neurological significance of this in the next chapter. Here I wish only to point out that if I am right in denying the presence of intellect and concept-formation in animals other than man, other animals always have agnosia, whereas in man it is an abnormality.

I think that what has been said so far suffices to tip the scales heavily on the side of man's differing in kind from other animals, rather than just differing in degree. But it does not resolve the issue fully if it can still be said that that difference in kind is superficial rather than radical because it rests solely on a difference in degree between the human brain and nervous apparatus and that of other animals.

It is generally acknowledged that there are great and striking differences in degree, with regard to size, weight, and structural complexity, between human and animal brains. What is not generally agreed upon, however, is how the operations of the human mind, even granted that it has intellectual as well as sensory powers, stand in relation to the functioning of the human brain and other nervous apparatus. On the contrary, that question is a matter of intense and elaborate dispute to which I shall turn in the next chapter.

Regardless of how the issue about mind and brain is resolved, we cannot ignore or forget the remarkable differences between human and animal behavior that betoken the uniqueness of the human mind by virtue of its intellectual powers.

Only human beings live with the awareness of death and with the certain knowledge that they are going to die.

Only human beings use their minds to become artists, scientists, historians, philosophers, priests, teachers, lawyers, physicians, engineers, accountants, inventors, traders, bankers, and statesmen.

Only among human beings is there a distinction between those who behave ethically and those who are knaves, scoundrels, villains, and criminals.

Only among human beings is there any distinction between those who have mental health and those who suffer mental disease or have mental disabilities of one sort or another.

Only in the sphere of human life are there such institutions as schools, libraries, hospitals, churches, temples, factories, theaters, museums, prisons, cemeteries, and so on.

I mentioned at the beginning of this chapter a book I wrote entitled *The Difference of Man and the Difference It Makes*. The bibliography in that book includes two groups of authors with whom I took issue at that time and with whom I undertook to argue. One group consisted of professors in the behavioral sciences who assert that man's mind differs only in degree, not in kind, from the mind of other animals, especially the higher mammals such as the anthropoid apes and the bottle-nosed dolphins. The other group consisted of computer technologists engaged in research on intelligent machines or what is called artificial intelligence (AI). I challenged their overconfident claim that they would be able to produce in the future machines capable of intelligent behavior that would equal or exceed the performances of the human mind.*

---

*If the reader is interested in a more up-to-date bibliography of the books with which I disagree, it can be found in Patricia Smith Churchland's *Neurophilosophy, Toward a Unified Science of the Mind-Brain* (1986). That bibliography, in very small type, runs to over thirty-three pages.

One point established clearly and forcefully in another book I wrote, *Ten Philosophical Mistakes* (1985), bears repetition here because it completes the answer to the question we have been considering. I have given many reasons for concluding that animals other than humans do not have intellects. I have also indicated many of the distinctive features of human life and behavior that it would be difficult to explain without reference to man's intellectual powers. But I have not so far mentioned one aspect of human behavior that simply *cannot* be explained without attributing intellect to man—a power that is radically distinct from and superior to all of our sensitive powers, our powers of sense-perception, sensitive memory, and imagination.

That crucial aspect of human behavior is our use of general terms—all of the common nouns in our vocabulary that name kinds or classes of things, some of which have perceptible instances and some of which do not.

Everything perceptible, memorable, and imaginable is a particular individual thing, an attribute of that thing, or an occurrent event. We can, for example, perceive visible figures that are triangles of a particular shape and size; we can also imagine or remember particular triangles. But we cannot by means of our sensitive powers think of triangularity in general, triangularity not particularized by shape, size, or color. Yet we use the word "triangle" and all the other general terms in our vocabulary with understanding of the universals—the kinds or classes of things—to which our general terms refer.

Our use of general terms that refer to universal objects of thought would be absolutely impossible if we did not have intellects able to do what our senses cannot do. This is the most conclusive reason for attributing to the human mind an intellectual power that is radically distinct from all of our sensitive powers and from the sensitive powers of other animals.

Philosophers who call themselves nominalists deny the existence of universal objects of thought. In doing so, they are in effect denying the existence of intellect as radically distinct from the senses. They try to explain our significant use of general terms or common names without permitting their significance to be construed as referring to anything except particulars—never to anything that is universal.

They try in vain because it cannot be done. Nominalism is self-refuting. This I have shown in chapter 3 of *Ten Philosophical Mistakes*. The argument set forth there need not be repeated here. For our present purposes, it suffices to close by saying that the refutation of nominalism (in fact, the self-refuting character of it) is the conclusive step in the establishment of the distinctive intellectual power of the human mind.

CHAPTER 4

Is Intellect Immaterial?

As PREPARATION for teaching psychology I studied neuroanatomy and neurophysiology in the early 1920s at Columbia University's College of Physicians and Surgeons. I became so fascinated with neurological science that, ever since then, I have followed its outstanding research contributions and the progress that has been made in our understanding of the nervous system.

The developments since World War II have been revolutionary. I taught my students that the brain was an elaborate electrical network with a vast number of cells and connections. We have now come to understand the brain as a chemical factory in which the messages transmitted are electrochemical. It is much less like an ordinary computer than it was once thought to be.

The brain's many chemical products are facilitators of the impulses that move across its nerve fibers. We know now that biochemical disturbances in the brain account for some mental disorders. From the extraordinary advances in research in the last twenty years, we have every reason to expect breakthroughs in our understanding of how the brain works that we cannot foresee at present.

At the same time, we must confess that there is much we do not understand, especially about the brain's relation to the mind. We do not understand, for example, why the transmission of nervous impulses from the external sense-organs does not result in conscious experience until these impulses activate the cerebral cortex. A blockage that would prevent their passage from the lower and midbrain connecting centers to the cerebral cortex would prevent awarenesses of colors, sounds, or smells that stimulated the external sense-organs.

Even more puzzling is the fact that when nervous impulses coming from the eyes reach the occipital area of the cerebral cortex, we see shapes and colors; when coming from the ears, they reach the temporal area and we hear sounds. These impulses, so far as we know, are the same in character; the nervous structure of the two cortical areas mentioned are also the same. Why, then, should there be a qualitatively different result in our conscious experience?

Neither do we understand the neurological basis of the agnosia that leaves a person able to see the shape and color of a rose held before his eyes, yet not be able to recognize that it is a rose until the rose is held under his nose to smell.

Both the visual and the olfactory organs seem to be working perfectly. The understanding of what a rose is has not been lost. What is malfunctioning in the brain that prevents understanding from being elicited by the sight of the rose when it is so readily elicited by the smell of it? We do not know.

There is much that we have yet to learn regarding the brain's relation to the mind in the field of sensory experience. But how much greater is our ignorance of the brain's relation to the mind in the sphere of intellectual activity? This does not mean that we will never have the knowledge we now lack. Further progress in neurology may achieve it, *but only if whatever happens in the mind can be fully explained by what happens in the brain.*

That *if* raises the questions to which we must now address ourselves. One is a question about the inseparability of mind and brain and the extent to which they may be distinct from one another. Another is a question about the dependence of the mind upon the brain and the extent to which mind may be independent of the brain.

The issue with which we are concerned is often poorly stated in the literature of the subject because the word "identity" is misused. Strictly speaking, if two things can be distinguished in any way, even if it is only by the fact of their twoness, they are not identical. Two ball bearings that are alike in every respect except the space each occupies at a given time cannot properly be called identical, though the word is often misused that way, as it is also misused when we speak of identical twins.

One extremist theory about mind and brain asserts their identity. Used literally, the word "identity" must here mean that there is no distinction whatsoever between mind and brain. That, in turn, means that the two words— "mind" and "brain"—are strict synonyms. If that is the case, we cannot meaningfully ask about the relation of psychology to neurology because psychology is identical with neurology.

Eliminating that troublesome word "identity" from our discussion, I propose to proceed in a way that I think clarifies the issue. It is a double-barreled issue involving two pairs of contrary views in such opposition to one another that both cannot be true but both can be false.

The first pair of opposed views I regard as going to opposite extremes, and, in my judgment, both are false. The opposed views in the second pair are more moderate: each has some truth in it, yet both cannot be completely true. If one is completely true, the other must be false, and it is possible that both may be false.

Let me deal with the two extremist views first, the falsity of which can be easily shown. In our philosophical vocabulary we have two "ism" words to name them. The words are "dualism" and "monism" and they at once suggest to us what is being said about mind and brain by the dualist, on the one hand, and by the monist, on the other hand.

In the history of thought about mind and brain, or body and soul, Plato and Descartes are the outstanding psychophysical dualists. They assert that man is constituted by two utterly distinct and existentially separate substances—for Plato, body and soul; for Descartes, matter and mind, extended substance and thinking substance. Strictly speaking, a human being is not what common sense supposes that person to be: one indivisible thing. That person is actually divided into two individual things, as different and distinct as the rower and the rowboat in which he sits.*

If this dualistic theory were true, it would confront us with the most embarrassing, insoluble difficulties should we try to explain how these two utterly different substances could interact with one another, as they appear to do in human behavior. Fortunately, the riddles of the mind-body problem that have plagued modern philosophy since Descartes can be dismissed. Two incontrovertible facts, which are matters of general knowledge, suffice for the refutation of psychophysical dualism.

One is the fact that we fall asleep from time to time. For some portion of the time that we are asleep, our minds are

---

*When we repeat the schoolbook syllogism "All men are mortal, Socrates is a man, therefore Socrates is mortal," what does the proper name "Socrates" refer to? In Platonic terms, Socrates has a mortal, perishable body and an immortal, imperishable soul. If the one word "Socrates" refers ambiguously to the two quite different individual things, then we cannot correctly conclude that Socrates is mortal, for only the physical Socrates—his body—is mortal, and the spiritual Socrates—his soul—is immortal.

totally inactive. We are unconscious. We know that sleep is induced by fatigue toxins that affect the brain. It can also be induced by drugs and pills. But if the mind is totally independent of the brain, then why should one brain condition allow for consciousness and another bring about unconscious sleep?

The second fact, equally well known to us, is that brain injuries or defects produce mental disabilities or disorders. We also have the reports from neurological surgery that tell of electrical stimulation of the brain producing conscious experiences. How can this be so if mind and brain are as separate as the rower and the rowboat, a separation so complete that it permits the rowboat to be sunk while the rower swims away unharmed?

The theory of the monist is at the diametrically opposite extreme. In earlier times it was called materialistic monism because it asserted that matter and matter alone exists—that the world consists of nothing but bodies and their motions. In the present century it has come to be called the identity hypothesis, misusing, as we have seen, the word "identity."

Materialistic monism that reductively identifies mind with brain cannot retain distinct meanings for the two words "mind" and "brain." The reduction of mind to brain totally excludes mind and the mental from consideration. There is nothing to talk or think about except the brain, its activities, its states, and its processes. The reductive materialist should expunge from his vocabulary the word "mind" and all the other words that go with it.

Can these words be expunged from his or anyone else's vocabulary and still allow us to describe experiences that everyone has? If not, then mind and brain are at least analytically distinct, even if they are existentially one and the same thing.

Toast and butter are existentially separate when each lies on a separate plate. When hot toast is buttered, the two become inseparable, but when the buttered toast is eaten, it still remains possible to distinguish by taste the butter from the toast.

Mind and brain may be existentially inseparable, and so regarded as one and the same thing, yet the mental and the physical may still be analytically distinct aspects of it. This can be put to the test in the following manner. Let a surgeon open up an individual's brain for inspection while the patient remains conscious. Let the surgeon dictate to a secretary his detailed observation of the visible area of the brain under scrutiny, and let that area of the brain be its center for vision. Let the patient dictate to another secretary a detailed description of the visible walls of the room in which the surgery is occurring.

The language used by the surgeon and the language used by the patient will be irreducibly different: the one will contain words referring to physical phenomena occurring in the brain; the other, words referring to conscious experiences of the room. The extreme monism that asserts not only the existential unity of brain and mind, but also that there is no analytical distinction between them, thus becomes untenable.

With both extremes eliminated, I turn now to the other more moderate pair of contrary views about the relation of mind to brain. Here there is no question about the analytical distinction between mental and physical acts, states, and processes. Both of the opposed views agree on that score but differ with regard to the dependence of the mental on the physical.

One view maintains that the activation of the brain and of other nervous processes is both the necessary and the sufficient condition for the occurrence of all mental states and of all the mind's acts and processes. This theory can be called materialistic, but it is not a reductive materialism.

The other view agrees in part and disagrees in part. With regard to certain sensory experiences, it agrees that the action of the brain and nervous system is both a necessary and a sufficient condition for their occurrence. But it disagrees when it comes to the intellectual activity of the mind in conceptual thought, and in any other activity that involves conceptual understanding, as in human sense-perception when the individual is not suffering from agnosia.

At this point, sharp disagreement arises. Here the nonmaterialistic view maintains that brain action is only a necessary, but not a sufficient, condition for the occurrence of the mental acts under consideration. If this is so, then some other factor—an immaterial factor—must be added. If we call the first of these two theories a moderate materialism, because it is not reductive and affirms at least the analytical distinction of the physical and the mental, then perhaps we may call the second, contrary theory a moderate immaterialism.

In the current state of this dispute, those who espouse the view I have called a moderate materialism tend to concentrate on sensory acts and processes in their effort to show that the brain is all that is needed for such mental acts and processes to occur. They give little attention to intellectual processes and conceptual thought, and ignore or overlook the involvement of concepts in sense-perception, memory, and imagination; or they attempt to explain these intellectual processes in terms that require no distinction between the senses and the intellect as separate cognitive powers.

In defending the opposed theory, which I have called a moderate immaterialism, the argument appeals mainly to what is required for intellectual activity and conceptual thought. Its central contention is that intellectual acts and processes cannot be explained in sensory terms and that more than the brain or any other material organ is required for them to occur

To say that the brain is only a necessary, but not a sufficient condition, is to say that we *cannot* think conceptually *without* our brains, but that we *do not* think conceptually *with* our brains. The brain is not the organ of thought as the eye and the brain together are the organs of vision, or the ear and brain together are the organs of hearing.

There is another way of saying this. As the eye or ear, together with the brain, are sense-organs, the brain itself is not a mind-organ; or, more precisely, the brain is not an intellect-organ. The most that can be said of the brain in relation to the human mind is that it is an intellect-support organ, an organ upon which the intellect depends, without which it cannot think, but with which it does not think.

Which of the two moderate but contrary views of the relation of mind to brain is correct determines how we answer the question that was left hanging at the end of the preceding chapter. If moderate materialism is correct, then the difference in kind that follows from the uniqueness of the human mind by virtue of its intellectual powers may be only a superficial difference in kind because all the extraordinarily wide differences between human and animal life, human and animal behavior, can be explained by differences in degree between human and animal brains.

Only if the brain is not the sufficient condition for intellectual activity and conceptual thought (only if the intellect that is part of the human mind and is not found in other animals is the immaterial factor that must be added to the brain in order to provide conditions both necessary and sufficient) are we justified in concluding that the manifest difference in kind between human and animal minds, and between human and animal behavior, is radical, not superficial. It cannot be explained away by any difference in the physical constitution of human beings and other animals that is a difference in degree.

I will try, as briefly as possible, to summarize the argument that I think supports the view that the intellect is the immaterial factor needed, in addition to the brain, for the occurrence in the human mind of conceptual thought. The argument, *as stated*, is not to be found in the philosophical

INTELLECT: MIND OVER MATTER   49

writings of Aristotle and Thomas Aquinas, but its main
tenets can be found there.

The argument hinges on two propositions. The first asserts that the concepts whereby we understand what different kinds or classes of things are like consist of meanings
that are universal. The second proposition asserts that nothing that exists physically is ever actually universal. Anything
that is embodied in matter exists as an individual, a singular
thing that may also be a particular instance of this class
or that.

From these two propositions, the conclusion follows that
our concepts, having universality, cannot be embodied in
matter. If they were acts of a bodily organ such as the brain,
they would exist in matter, and so could not have the
requisite universality to function as concepts that enable us
to think of universal objects, such as kinds or classes, quite
different from the individual things that are objects of sense-
perception, imagination, and memory. The power of conceptual thought, by which we form and use concepts, must,
therefore, be an immaterial power, one the acts of which are
not acts of a bodily organ.

The reasoning that supports the first of the two foregoing propositions is as follows. Our common or general
names derive the meanings they carry from the concepts we
have. The meaning of a common or general name is universal. It always signifies a class of objects, never any particular
instance or member of the class. Particular instances are
designated by proper names or definite descriptions. When we
use the word "dog," we are referring to any dog, regardless
of breed, size, shape, or color. To refer to a particular instance,
we would use a canine name, such as "Fido," or a definite
description, such as "that white poodle over there lying in
front of the fire." Our concepts of dog and poodle not only
enable us to think about two classes of animals, they also
enable us to understand what it is like to be a dog or a poodle.

The second proposition about the individuality of all material or corporeal things is supported by the facts of common experience. The objects we perceive through our senses are all individual things—that is, this individual dog, that individual spoon. As I pointed out in the preceding chapter, we have never seen a triangle in general, nor can we imagine one. Any triangle that we can draw on a piece of paper, any triangle we have seen or imagined, is a particular triangle of a certain shape and size. But we can understand what is involved in triangularity as such, without reference to the character of the angles or the area enclosed.

Whatever exists physically exists as an individual, and whatever has individuality exists materially. No one has ever experienced or produced anything that has physical or corporeal existence and also is universal in character rather than individual.

The argument then reaches its conclusion as follows. Our concepts are universal in their signification of objects that are kinds or classes of things rather than individuals that are particular instances of these classes or kinds. Since they have universality, they cannot exist physically or be embodied in matter. But concepts do exist in our minds. They are there as acts of our intellectual power. Hence that power must be an immaterial power, not one embodied in a material organ such as the brain.

The action of the brain, therefore, cannot be the sufficient condition of conceptual thought, though it may still be a necessary condition thereof, insofar as the exercise of our power of conceptual thought depends on the exercise of our powers of perception, memory, and imagination, which are corporeal powers cmbodied in our sense-organs and brain.

If it can be shown that any other animal, such as the dolphin, has the power of conceptual thought, the argument just stated would lead to the same conclusion about the dolphin: namely, that it has an immaterial power and that the action of the dolphin brain is only a necessary, but not a sufficient, condition of the occurrence of conceptual thought on the part of the dolphin.

I have just summarized the bare bones of the argument, but readers may wish to put its premises to the test.

First, attempt to explain the general significance of the common nouns in our vocabulary, the significance of which is so different from the designative reference of the proper names we use, without appealing to our conceptual understanding of classes or kinds to which perceived or imagined particulars belong. If you cannot do that, then our apprehension of universals—of classes or kinds—is indispensable to our understanding of the meaning of common nouns or names.

Our cognitive sensory powers do not and cannot apprehend universals. Their cognitive reach does not go beyond particulars. Hence, we would not be able to apprehend universals if we did not have another and quite distinct cognitive power—the power of intellect.

Then ask yourself whether the particular individual things you apprehend by sense-perception or imagination are always bodies or the attributes of bodies, never anything the existence of which is incorporeal or immaterial. When you open your eyes and look out the window, what do you see? This or that individual tree; this or that automobile; this or that particular building. Whatever it is, it is always some physical thing, some material embodiment. When you close your eyes and let your imagination roam, what do you then apprehend? The same again: always some individual, physical thing; some material embodiment.

The fact that the world we perceive through our senses and all the things we can imagine and remember are individual physical things or material embodiments gives great credibility to the materialistic thesis that the world of real existences is entirely material, that nothing immaterial really exists.

The great credibility of that thesis does not make the proposition self-evidently true, nor does it constitute proof of its truth. The proposition, however credible, still remains a postulate that should not be dogmatically asserted as an indubitable truth—true beyond the shadow of a doubt.

What has just been said not only challenges the dogmatism of the materialist; it also, paradoxically, reveals the reasons why the materialistic dogma is so credible to all of us as well as the grounds for asserting the immateriality of the intellect.

Why do we find the materialistic dogma so credible? Because the world of our sense-experience and of our imagination and memory is filled with nothing but individual objects all of which are physical bodies, material things or their attributes.

At the same time, the individual physical things in the world of our sense-experience are also particular instances of certain kinds or classes of things—the kinds or classes to which the common names or general terms we use refer. We could not use those words with their general significance if we were not able to apprehend the objects of conceptual thought—the intelligible, universal objects that only our intellects can apprehend.

Readers are thus led to the conclusion that the power by which we apprehend those intelligible objects, those universal objects of conceptual thought, must be immaterial. For if the concepts by which we apprehend such objects were acts of bodily organs, their material embodiment would prevent them from being apprehensions of anything universal. They would, in this respect, be no different from the percepts and the images that are acts of bodily organs (the sense-organs and the brain) and, therefore, are always apprehensions of individual things or of their particular attributes.

We are not done yet. It was pointed out earlier that the two extreme theories of psychophysical dualism and materialistic monism can both be false, though both cannot be true. We must now acknowledge that the same applies to the two moderate theories: the theory that the brain is not only a necessary but also a sufficient condition of all mental acts and processes; and the theory that the brain is only a necessary, but not a sufficient, condition of conceptual thought, that an immaterial intellect is also required and must be posited in order to provide an adequate explanation of conceptual thought. These moderate theories cannot both be true, but both can be false.

Even if both are false, we are left with one solid conclusion, which is the one point on which both of these moderate theories concur: namely, that there is at least an analytical distinction between mental and physical acts and processes. That being the case, our understanding of the intellectual powers of the human mind can be stated in purely mental terms. It does not depend on our knowledge of the brain, nor does it depend on how we view the intellect's relation to the brain.

Thus, for example, the clear difference between perceptual and conceptual thought, which is so important in understanding the difference between animal and human behavior, remains unchanged by the adoption of one rather than the other of the two conflicting theories. It remains the same whether we view conceptual thought as an act of the brain or of an immaterial intellectual power. What is affected by taking one or another of these alternative moderate views is only whether the difference in kind between human and animal behavior is a superficial or a radical difference in kind.

Lest readers are misled by the foregoing summation, let me clearly reiterate the position that I think I have shown to be demonstrably true: that the brain is only a necessary, but not a sufficient, condition for conceptual thought; that an immaterial intellect is also requisite as a condition; and that the difference between human and animal behavior is a radical difference in kind.

CHAPTER 5

Artificial Intelligence
and the Human Intellect

CURRENTLY many behavioral scientists accept the prediction that computer technology will make it possible to construct machines with artificial intelligence that will enable them to do everything that human beings can do. Their performance will be indistinguishable from that of the human intellect. Underlying this prediction is the materialistic dogma that denies the immateriality of the human intellect—the dogma that supports the view that the brain is the necessary and sufficient condition of all mental acts and processes.

These projected artificial intelligence machines will not be alive, will have no vegetative powers, and, while they may have something like the sensory powers of living organisms, especially perceptive powers, they will not have consciousness or experience feelings of pleasure and pain or the emotions of anger and fear.

If all the apparent differences in kind between human and animal behavior are only superficial, in the sense that they can all be explained by a vast difference in degree of structural complexity between the human brain and the brains of other animals, then the materialistic dogma has obvious grounds in support of its prediction.

The present differences in the degree of structural complexity between the human brain and that of artificial intelligence machines can certainly be overcome in the future. There is no reason to suppose that machines cannot be constructed with parallel processing and with structural components and connections in excess of 10^{11}, which is the measure of the human brain's structural complexity. Artificial intelligence machines will then be as intellectually competent as we are. It may even be that the performance of these future machines will clearly surpass the best human efforts and accomplishments.

At present, the most powerful and intricate machines can do many things that brute animals cannot do, as well as many things that human beings can do, such as mathematical calculations, all forms of logical reasoning, and heuristic formulations. In addition, those machines can do these things better than many human beings, and more quickly than most. Their use in putting a man on the moon is a striking example of this. That could not have been done without them.

However, they cannot do some of the things that almost all human beings can do, especially those flights of fancy, those insights attained without antecedent logical thought, those innovative yet nonrational leaps of the mind.

Even the most optimistic computer technologists are willing to admit this while they remain confident in predicting the success of their efforts in the future. That confidence rests on their dogmatically asserted materialistic assumption that everything depends on the size and structural complexity of the brain and nervous system in human beings and of the material components and connections in the machines they hope to build in the future.

The declaration of the seventeenth century by the French philosopher René Descartes that *matter cannot think* is the battle cry of those who deny that the technologists' prediction will ever come true. The technologists' battle cry is just the opposite: matter can be made to think in all the ways that human beings think. Their thesis is the very opposite of the thesis of this book: not mind over matter, but matter over mind.

Since the position one takes on this issue depends on one's position regarding the intellect's immateriality, it may be used to open this chapter on artificial intelligence with answers to the objections that have been and can be raised against the thesis that the brain is only a necessary, but not the sufficient, condition of conceptual thought, and that an immaterial intellect as a component of the human mind is required in addition to the brain as a necessary condition.

First objection and reply. The clinical data of brain pathology, especially brain injuries that are accompanied by disorders of speech and by the loss of understanding, show the involvement of the brain in the processes of conceptual thought, just as other brain injuries causing blindness or deafness show the involvement of the brain in perceptual processes. Hence the one set of processes like the other must be a function of the brain. This objection was met by Aquinas in the thirteenth century. He dealt with the impediments to conceptual thought that result from brain injuries as well as the interference that results from the effect of toxic substances and fatigue poisons on the action of the brain.

Aquinas pointed out that there is no inconsistency between admitting the involvement of the brain in conceptual thought and asserting the intellect's immateriality. All that the evidence from brain pathology shows is that the brain is a necessary condition of conceptual thought, and in order to deny that the brain is the sufficient condition of conceptual thought, one does not have to deny that it is a necessary condition.

The error of the objection consists in treating conceptual and perceptual processes as wholly alike in being functions of the brain—that is, in treating *visual* blindness (loss of sight) as if it were the same as *conceptual* blindness or agnosia (loss of understanding). To treat them as the same is to ignore the argument for the immateriality of conceptual thought. The objection can hardly invalidate an argument that it ignores.

Second objection and reply. The human infant is not born able to exercise the power of propositional speech. It is only in the course of maturation that that power comes into operation and develops with exercise. The infant's first use of names or designators and his first utterance of sentences do not occur until, with growth, his brain reaches a certain magnitude. Hence it would appear that there is a critical threshold in the continuum of brain magnitudes above which the human being has and below which he lacks propositional speech. Since the presence of propositional speech is our only objective evidence of the presence of conceptual thought, it can be argued that engaging in conceptual thought depends, as engaging in propositional speech also depends, on a certain brain magnitude.

The reply to this objection, like the reply to the preceding one, concedes that conceptual thought depends on the brain, and especially on its having a certain magnitude. However, all this shows is that the brain, or a certain magnitude of it, is a necessary condition of conceptual thought. The argument for the immateriality of conceptual thought, the whole point of which is to show that the brain is not the sufficient condition of conceptual thought, remains untouched by this objection.

Third objection and reply. It has been conceded that animals and machines are capable of perceptual abstractions. Rats can learn to react to different triangles *as if* they all had some characteristic in common (their triangularity) that is not shared by other visible shapes; some success has been achieved in getting machines to recognize different shapes in an apparently discriminating manner (i.e., react in one way to square shapes, and in another to triangular shapes). It would thus appear that animals and machines are able to apprehend universals—classes or kinds of objects. But unless an immaterial power is to be attributed to subhuman animals and to machines, it would seem to follow that an immaterial power need not be posited to explain man's apprehension of classes or kinds of objects. Hence, even if it is granted that the concepts whereby we know kinds or classes are universal intentions, that does not justify our positing the immateriality of the power of conceptual thought.

The reply to this objection hinges on preserving the distinction between perceptual abstraction and concept formation. A perceptual abstraction, as attained by men or other animals, is an acquired disposition to perceive a number of sensible particulars as being of the same kind or as sufficiently similar to be reacted to in the same way; it is also a disposition to discriminate between similar and dissimilar particulars. It is not a disposition to recognize a single perceived particular as being of a certain kind, for the recognition of a single perceived particular as being of a certain kind is inseparable from the understanding of the kind itself. These related acts of recognition and understanding presuppose more than perceptual abstraction; they presuppose concept-formation. For a laboratory rat that has learned a food cue, a perceptual abstraction or generalization enables it to perceive that this shape and this shape (e.g., triangular shapes) but not this shape or that (e.g., circular shapes) are sufficiently alike to serve as the cue for a certain response.

But such perceptual generalization and discrimination does not dispose the rat to recognize that this shape by itself is a triangle or to understand triangularity when no triangular shapes are perceptually present. Only man, having the concept of triangularity, can recognize this perceived shape as being an instance of triangularity, and can, in the absence of any perceived shape, understand triangularity and the distinction between it and circularity.

By means of a perceptual abstraction, like that attained by the laboratory rat, man can also perceive a number of sensible particulars as similar shapes and discriminate between them and dissimilar shapes, but his recognition that the similar shapes are all triangles and that the dissimilar shapes are circles derives from his concepts of triangle and circle, which operate in conjunction with his perceptual abstractions.*

The central point here is that perceptual abstractions do not function in the same way in man, on the one hand, and in nonlinguistic animals and machines, on the other hand. In man they operate in conjunction with concepts; in other animals and machines, they do not. It is only through concepts that we are able to understand kinds or classes of objects, and it is only through concepts in conjunction with perceptual abstractions that we are able to recognize this

---

*Without concepts, we would only perceive, as animals do, the individual thing. If we reacted to a number of individually differing things in the same way, we would not be cognizing what is common to them or knowing them in their universal aspects; we would only be reacting to them as functionally equivalent stimuli. By means of concepts, and only by means of concepts, we understand kinds or classes as such entirely apart from perceived particulars and even though no particular instances exist. By means of percepts alone—*if that ever occurs in human cognition*—we would apprehend individual things without any understanding of them. This is the meaning of Kant's statement that percepts without concepts are blind, and concepts without percepts empty. Hence, if we are right in thinking that men have and other animals lack the power of conceptual thought, then we must also assert a difference in kind between perceptual processes in animals, which are blind in Kant's sense, and perceptual processes in men, which are enlightened by concepts.

perceived object as being of a certain kind or class that we understand.

Perceptual abstractions by themselves, functioning in the absence of concepts as they do in animals and machines, can do no more than enable the animal or machine to discriminate between perceived particulars according to whether they are sufficiently alike or sufficiently different to warrant a particular reaction.

It might be difficult for anyone to say which of three technological innovations in the twentieth century, other than the harnessing of atomic energy, has had the most profound effect on human life: the motor car, the airplane, or the computer. But I have no hesitation in saying that, with regard to our understanding of man and his mind, the computer is not only foremost but stands alone. The centuries-old controversies about the questions and issues raised in the preceding chapters have taken a new turn because of the promise or threat of what might be accomplished by machines in the future.

Computers of the latest generation and machines that are devised to be embodiments of artificial intelligence (hereafter referred to as AI machines) have done remarkable things, and not merely in the performance of mathematical operations but also in playing games like chess, in problem-solving, in perceptual performances, in the processes of learning, and in making decisions. With regard to these accomplishments, three points should be reiterated.

First, computers are able to do what no animal, even those nearest to man in the scale of intelligence, can do at all. If the question that we asked about man and brute—Do they differ in kind or in degree?—were asked about computers and animals other than man, there could be no doubt about the answer: clearly in kind. This explains why technologists concerned with constructing AI machines have no interest in simulating animal behavior, only human performances.

Second, when computers do what human beings can do, they do it with much greater speed and much greater accuracy, and often in magnitudes of complexity that exceed the reach of human beings. It would have been impossible, for example, to put a man on the moon without the use of computers.

Third, the difference in degree that exists at present with regard to the size and complexity of computers and human brains is still vast. The number of cells in the human brain is estimated to be 10^{11}, and the number of their interconnections is much greater than that. The number of transistor components in the largest computer so far constructed is 10^3 or 10^4 at the most. However, it is certainly both possible and even likely that computers built in the future will have componentry and interconnections in their circuitry that exceed what can be found in the human brain.

This last fact might lead us to suppose that when this happens, it should also be possible to build AI machines that will outperform human beings in all the things human beings can do and no other animal can do at all. If we jumped to that conclusion, we might then suppose that we had resolved the issue about whether the difference in kind between human and animal behavior was superficial or radical.

That supposition would be false because we had jumped too fast, we did not consider all the relevant alternatives. If the conclusion I argued for in the preceding chapter, as well as in the opening pages of the present chapter, is correct, then whatever progress is made in the future of computer technology, it will remain true that no AI machine ever to be constructed will be able to perform in a manner that is indistinguishable from human performance.

My argument, however, may have flaws in it, and I conceded that possibility when I said that while the contrary views cannot both be true, they can both be false. If my defense of the view that an immaterial factor must be present in order for there to be conceptual thought is not a sound one, then we cannot say it is impossible for an AI machine to be built that will be able to do everything the human mind can do.

Should that possibility ever be realized, the issue would be finally resolved beyond all reasonable doubt. We know that the AI machine is a purely material contraption. No immaterial factor enters into its construction. Hence, if it should demonstrate its ability to do everything the human mind can do, we would be compelled to conclude that the brain and nervous system with no immaterial factor added is not only necessary but also sufficient for all our mental activities, including the highest reaches of conceptual thought. That conclusion would carry with it the additional conclusion that the difference in kind between human beings and other animals is only superficial, not radical.

I hope I have made quite clear how crucially important is the role that AI machines can play with regard to the problems we have been considering. I hope it is also quite clear that, at this moment, we do not know which way the dice will fall. The failure of future AI machines to simulate every aspect of human behavior will be just as significant one way as their success will be the other way.

The future AI machine that will be put to the test of its power to *simulate* human behavior need not *replicate* the functioning of the human nervous system.* Unless "wet computers" are built, in which the impulses transmitted are

*We must distinguish between simulation and what is called "replication." The attempts to construct mechanical models that operate in the same way the human brain operates are efforts at replication. In contrast to replication, the simulation of human behavior by machines consists in achieving the same end result in the way of performance but not achieving it in the same way. Thus, for example, airplanes simulate the flight of birds, but the mechanics of flight are not the same in both cases, though both bird and airplane obey the same laws of aerodynamics.

electrochemical, not purely electrical, achieving the same end result but not achieving it in the same way will suffice.

The fact that the AI machine is not a living organism, does not laugh or weep, is not subject to moods, nor manifests any nonintellectual aspects of human conduct has no bearing on the outcome of the test. We are concerned here only with how intelligent machines compare with the *power* of the human intellect, and not just with human intelligence.

The challenge to future technologists is very precise. It does not call for the production of an AI machine the performance of which will provide us with an answer to the loose and unclear question, "Can machines think?" In its use by psychologists, neurologists, computer technologists, and philosophers, the word "think" has so many meanings in its application to animals, man, and machines that if anyone asks "Can animals think?" or "Can machines think?" the answer will be "yes" in some senses of the word and "no" in others.

Fortunately, in order to make a critical test of artificial or machine intelligence, *it is only necessary to do what is possible*—namely, gain general acceptance of a definition of human thinking in all its variety. A test can be devised that involves a distinctively human performance, one that the AI machine must succeed in simulating. The human performance in question is that of conversation. As a defender of man's distinctive capacity for conceptual thought, I would be quite satisfied with that as a test of a machine's comparable intellectual capacity.

When Descartes declared centuries ago that matter cannot think, he challenged his materialist opponents to construct a machine that could engage in conversation with a human being. If that could be done, he was prepared to admit his error. I would say the same thing today. If computer technologists can succeed in constructing a machine able to engage in conversation with a human being,

I, too, would admit error in the arguments I have so far
advanced.

One of the most eminent mathematicians among the
computer technologists of this century, Alan Turing, claimed
that it is, in principle, mathematically possible to construct a
machine able to pass this test. He went further and proposed a foolproof way to test his mathematically conceivable Turing machine.

Known as the Turing game, it involves substituting a
machine for either a man or a woman in the game. When
that game is played with a male and female human being, it
is played in the following manner: a man and woman are
placed behind a screen. An interrogator stands in front and
asks them questions in order to see if he can detect whether
the answers received come from the male or female behind
the screen. The persons behind the screen are permitted to
lie or to resort to any other trick that may help defeat the
interrogator's effort. The answers are delivered in written
form so that tone of voice does not reveal the gender of the
responder. When this game is played properly, the interrogator's chance of succeeding is fifty-fifty, which in Turing's
view indicates mere guessing and, therefore, failure for the
interrogator.

In Turing's version of this game, an AI machine is substi-
tuted for one of the two human beings. Behind the screen is
a human being and an AI machine. The interrogator asks
them questions to try to differentiate the human from the
machine responses, which are delivered, of course, in some
uniformly printed manner. Those behind the screen must try
to avoid detection by the way they answer the questions.

If the interrogator can succeed only at the level of chance
(only 50 percent of the time), he is judged to have failed and
the Turing machine is deemed successful. It has performed
in a manner indistinguishable from that of a human.

A slightly altered and, perhaps, simpler version of the
Turing game would involve a lengthy conversation between

two individuals, hidden from one another by a screen, with both questions and answers delivered in printed form. On one occasion the two individuals would both be human beings. On another occasion one of the two would be a Turing machine and the other would be the same human being.

If that person could not tell which of the two conversations involved another human being and which involved a machine, Turing's claim would be verified—that a machine can be constructed to perform in a manner indistinguishable from what is accepted as a distinctively human performance involving conceptual thought.

To construct a machine able to play the Turing game or to engage in conversation with a human being, a number of obstacles must be surmounted. In the first place, the machine's performance cannot be one that is completely programmed. Everything programmed is predictable; even a certain range of random behavior, if programmed, is predictable. But the Turing game involves questions from the interrogator that are unpredictable by any programmer; so, too, are the turns and twists in a long conversation conducted by human beings.

The Turing machine, therefore, cannot have the kind of programming used in an ordinary computer. It may have what Turing calls "infant programming"—some fixed connections like the innate reflexes possessed by a human infant at birth. The Turing machine must also be able to operate through flexible and random connections. It must, in other words, be able to learn and be teachable; beyond that, for the purposes of playing the Turing or conversational game, it must be able to acquire the use of a natural language, such as English, which includes common nouns that are names with universal significance.

At birth, human beings are endowed with the ability to learn from experience, and especially the ability to learn any language whatsoever, as well as the ability to think about any subject whatsoever within the range of all possible thinkables. If such native endowment is regarded as programming, quite different from the kind of programming now put into computers, then a Turing machine that succeeded would have to be programmed in this way, not as computers are now programmed.

Holding the view that I have so far expressed—that the brain is not the organ of thought and that an immaterial factor in the human mind is required in order for its universal concepts to confer significance on the general terms we use in ordinary discourse—I regard it as highly improbable that a Turing machine will ever be built that is able to succeed in passing the Turing test.

Highly improbable does not mean impossible. To get at the truth about this matter, it is of the utmost importance for computer technologists to keep on trying to produce the machine that Turing claimed is, in principle, mathematically possible.*

Philosophical arguments frequently fail to persuade the opponents at which they are directed. I have good reason to doubt that the arguments I have directed against the moderate materialists at the end of the preceding chapter and at the beginning of this one will persuade them that the brain may be the necessary, but cannot be the sufficient, condition of conceptual thought.

How else might they be persuaded of the soundness of my view, if in fact it is correct? By the failure of the computer technologists to build the requisite AI machine—one that can perform as Turing claimed it should be able to. Each time the technologists try and fail, the possibility of their success becomes less and less probable. Each successive

---

*On this point, see the argument to the contrary in a book by a mathematical physicist who is also a philosopher: *Brain, Mind, and Computers* (1969) by Professor Stanley L. Jaki. The book was awarded the Le comte du Nouy Prize for 1970.

failure increases the probability that machines will never be able to perform in a manner indistinguishable from that of the human mind.

The answer may not be forthcoming in the immediate future, but the pursuit of truth is an unending process involving the whole of available time. Up to the present moment, machines have not turned in the requisite performance. Reasons can be given for thinking that they never will. I am content to let matters stand that way. I hope my readers feel the same.

CHAPTER 6

Extraterrestrial Intelligence

ARTIFICIAL INTELLIGENCE MACHINES are not the only twentieth-century innovation relevant to our discussion of the human mind and intellect. Another is the widely discussed hypothesis that a form of intelligent life will be found elsewhere in this cosmos besides earth.

It is interesting that those who favor this hypothesis claim that in our vast and ever-expanding universe, a form of intelligent life will be found not just on a few, or on a hundred, or even on a thousand other planets, but on millions of them. Those who oppose the hypothesis do not merely recommend caution about hypothesizing intelligent life elsewhere in the cosmos. Nor do they simply express doubts about the number of places where it may be found. They deny its existence entirely. The alternatives with which we are confronted are: none or millions.

We are not concerned with the respective merits of the opposing views or with the reasons or evidence offered in support of them. For our present purpose we are concerned only with two hypothetical questions, and they are:

68

1. IF intelligent life is found anywhere else in the cosmos, without regard to the number of planets on which it is found, will such extraterrestrial intelligence be essentially like human intelligence—a thinking mind with intellectual as well as sensory powers?

2. IF NOT, will it be instead on the level of brute animals, and so be *inferior* to human intelligence; or will it be *superior* to human intelligence by virtue of having cognitive and ratiocinative powers that surpass those of the human intellect—powers of a kind and magnitude with which we have no acquaintance at present?

My response to these two questions is definite only with respect to the last alternative. I think I can argue that if extraterrestrial intelligence is found elsewhere in the universe, it will *not* surpass human intelligence by virtue of having novel cognitive and ratiocinative powers not possessed by man. I think I can explain why a living, corporeal organism that is equipped with senses, memory, and imagination, and that also has bodily feelings and is subject to the turbulence of the emotions, cannot have cognitive and ratiocinative powers superior in kind to the powers of the human intellect.

The rest of that question I cannot answer definitely, nor can I support with reasonable arguments whatever conjectures I may harbor. I cannot say whether extraterrestrial intelligent beings, if they are found, will have powers essentially like our own; nor can I say that they will have inferior powers and so be on the same level as that of the brute animals on earth, equipped only with instincts and emotions and a range of sensory powers but totally lacking intellect.

These conjectures are not decisive with respect to other possibilities. The sensory powers of extraterrestrial living organisms may be different from those of human beings and of other earthly animals. To the extent that they are the same, they may be more or less acute, differing in degree from the powers we have or that are possessed by other animals on earth.

Readers will discern the assumption I am making. I am taking it for granted that if extraterrestrial intelligence is found on other planets, it will be found in corporeal living organisms, *not* totally disembodied or, if embodied, *not* in machines or robots. That assumption eliminates many of the fanciful characters of science fiction with which we need not be concerned.

In addition, the assumption I am making about extraterrestrial intelligence being embodied in living organisms employs the words "living," "organism," "corporeal," and "body" with exactly the same meanings we attach to them when we talk about terrestrial things. If the opposite were true, if we were to use these words equivocally so that when used of terrestrial and extraterrestrial beings they did not have the same meaning, then we would not know what we were talking about and would be engaging in the wildest of science fiction.

In short, I am saying that what it means to be alive, to have a body, to be equipped with senses, memory, and imagination, and to have an intellect must be the same in order for us to talk intelligibly and meaningfully about terrestrial and extraterrestrial beings.

Confining myself, as indicated above, to arguments for the one definite conclusion that is completely negative, I will try to show why it is very unlikely, if not impossible, for extraterrestrial living organisms to have cognitive and ratiocinative power superior in kind, not just in degree, to those of the human intellect.

The theoretical underpinnings of my argument have already been intimated earlier in this book. In chapter 1, in discussing the significance attached to the word "soul" in antiquity, I pointed out that having a soul was not thought to be peculiar to humans. Animals, too, and also plants have souls, for having a soul is simply equivalent to being alive. To be alive is to be besouled.

In this context I also pointed out that, in discussing soul, the ancients observed the three grades of life with which living organisms are endowed, derived from the fact that organic bodies have three grades of soul: (1) the vegetative soul that endows plants with the power to nourish, to grow, and to reproduce; (2) the sensitive soul that endows brute animals with all the foregoing vegetative powers and, in addition, all the powers of sense, appetite or desire, and of locomotion or of attachment to a place, as in sessile shellfish; and (3) the intellectual soul that endows human beings, in addition to all the powers possessed by plants and brute animals, with the rational powers of conceptual thought, judgment, ratiocination, deliberation, and decision with free choice among alternatives.

What should be immediately noted is that these three grades of life—vegetative, sensitive, and intellectual—constitute an ordering that is hierarchical. That ordering is like the order of the integers in arithmetic, or of the regular plane figures in geometry.

Consider the series constituted by triangle, square, and pentagon. In that ascending series, the second differs from the first by the addition of one angle, as does the third from the second. Furthermore, the square includes within its boundaries two triangles that can be found by drawing one diagonal; and the pentagon includes within its boundaries both a square and a triangle, which can be found also by drawing one diagonal.

The same kind of hierarchical ordering prevails among the three grades of life. Brute animals that have vegetative powers differ from plants that have these same powers by the addition of one other set of conjoined powers: sensitivity, appetition, and either local motion or occupation of place. Human beings that are rational animals have vegetative and sensitive powers, but they differ from other animals that are brute by the addition of a still further set of conjoined powers: all the intellectual powers of conceptual and rational thought.

This hierarchical ordering of the grades of life differs markedly from the scientific taxonomies employed in the classification of plants by botanists and of animals by zoologists. Such classifications involve many levels of generality from such lower level classes as species and genera up to higher level classes such as phyla, families, and orders. At the higher levels of the zoologist's taxonomy, or scheme of classification, we encounter such distinctions as those between unicellular and multicellular animals, between animals without backbones and those with; and among those with backbones, the distinctions that establish such classes as fish, reptiles, amphibians, birds, and mammals.

What is notable about this method of classification, as contrasted with the hierarchical ordering outlined above, is that in order to define distinct classes, it employs differences that are all positive and coordinate. Thus, for example, among vertebrates that have locomobility, some crawl; some walk; some swim; some fly; some fly and walk; some swim and walk; and some crawl, walk, and swim. Similarly, among mammals that have progeny, some reproduce viviparously by carrying the embryonic organism in utero and some reproduce oviparously by the laying of eggs.

This method of classification can be stated formally as follows. In the genus "X," two species of that genus are differentiated by two positive and coordinate differences "a" and "b." "Xa" and "Xb" are species of the genus "X," one neither higher nor lower than the other.

In contrast, the hierarchical ordering of the three grades of life is accomplished by another type of differentiation as follows. In the most comprehensive genus, that of all living organisms, plants have only one set of vital powers (the vegetative) and animals have that set of vital powers plus one additional set of powers (the sensitive). In consequence, plants can be defined *negatively* as nonsensitive vegetative living organisms. If "X" is used to represent the genus *living organisms,* and if "a" and "b" are used to represent vegetative and sensitive powers, then plants can be defined as "Xa, non-b" and animals can be defined as "Xa, b." Then, in the less comprehensive genus *animal living organisms,* using "c" to represent the intellectual powers, brute animals can be defined as "X, a, b, non-c." That leaves human animals to be defined as "X, a, b, c."

Plants are thus seen to be living organisms that have vegetative powers but lack sensitive and intellectual powers; brute animals are seen to be living organisms that have both vegetative and sensitive powers but lack intellectual powers; and human beings, at the summit of this hierarchical order, have all three sets of powers—vegetative, sensitive, and intellectual.

The hierarchical order is an ascending series of grades of life in which the higher grade always includes the powers possessed by the lower and surpasses it by the possession of one additional set of powers. The lower grade is always differentiated from the higher grade negatively by deprivation of a set of powers possessed by the higher grade.

In sharp contrast, the classifications employed by taxonomic botanists and zoologists tend for the most part to differentiate classes—species, genera, phyla, and so on—by contrary positive properties that render the classes thus differentiated *coordinate,* not higher and lower—not *supraordinate* and *subordinate* to one another.

If evolution and speciation were to continue in the millions of years that lie ahead on earth, and if this planet is not destroyed by a man-made cataclysm, nothing higher than human life would ever evolve. A higher grade of intelligence is conceivable, but to be a higher grade of intelligent life, a living being would have to have intellectual powers that are not limited by their dependence on the corporeal powers that are present in all animal life, including human life—dependence on the senses and on the passions.

The angelic intellect is a grade of intelligent life higher than human life, but angels, being incorporeal (minds *without* bodies, intellects totally separated from matter),* would not be organisms and would hardly be terrestrial creatures. For exactly the same reasons, they would not and could not exist anywhere in the physical, corporeal universe.

If, in addition to being quite conceivable by anyone who is not a dogmatic materialist, angels do have real existence in the universe (which is affirmed by religious faith but is not demonstrable by philosophical argument), their home is in heaven, which is not a physical place having the familiar dimensions of time and space.

In the hierarchical order of the grades of life, there is nothing intermediate between plant and animal life. Tropism in plants is quite distinct from sensation in animals. Nor is there anything intermediate between brute animal and human life, between the nonintellectual and the intellectual.

Each is a whole step up or down, as in the series of integers without intermediate fractions or, even more plainly, as in the series of rectilinear plane figures in geometry. There can be nothing intermediate between triangle and quadrangle, or between quadrangle and pentagon. Similarly, there is no grade of intelligent life that is intermediate between that of the human and that of the angelic intellect, superior in kind to the former and inferior in kind to the latter.

In order to have an intellect superior to the human intellect, it would be necessary to have one that is in no way

*For a fuller discussion of this, see my book *The Angels and Us* (1982).

dependent on the senses, the sensitive memory, and imagination; one that is not in any way affected by bodily feelings; one that is not in any way impeded in its operations by bodily emotions, or pushed blindly by the driving force of the passions. All these advantages can be enjoyed only by an intellect in total separation from a body—by the intellect of an angel, not by an intellect that belongs to a body and for which the necessary, though not the sufficient, condition of its functioning is the action of a brain and nervous system.

Plato and Descartes, who misconceived the human intellect as functionally independent of a body though mysteriously attached to one, committed what I have called an angelistic fallacy. This consists in attributing to the human intellect properties and powers that, if they have reality, could only be found in the angels in heaven, not in any earthly or extraterrestrial physical organism.*

If we avoid that angelistic fallacy, we are left with the conclusion that neither on earth nor anywhere else in the physical cosmos will there ever be found corporeal intelligent life that is superior in kind to the human intellect.

*The Angels and Us, chapters 9–10.

PART II

Serious Mistakes

CHAPTER 7

About Philosophy in Relation

to Common Sense

ARE OUR MINDS COGNITIVE—that is, are they instruments whereby we are able to acquire knowledge and attain understanding of the real world that is the same reality for all of us?

Is our experience of that reality sufficiently the same for all of us so that each of us can communicate about it with other human beings all over the globe?

Is there any need to prove the existence of an external world, one that has an independent reality, one that is the same whether we know it or not, and no matter how we know it?

Can a person who has learned to think in one language also learn to think in another of the many diverse human languages, and will the general tenor of that thinking be altered by the shift from one language to another?

Does the mentality of human beings differ with the diverse cultures in which we are reared and in which we live, or is the human mind basically the same throughout the world, differing only in superficial respects from one culture to another?

With the possible exception of the last question, persons of uninstructed—or should I say "unsophisticated"—common sense would without hesitation answer the first four questions with affirmations, unqualified by serious doubts. I say "uninstructed or unsophisticated common sense" in order to exclude those who have in one way or another been affected (I almost said "infected") by major strains in *modern* philosophical thought.

Before I explain my stress on the word "modern," I should, perhaps, apologize to my readers (all of whom I expect are persons of common sense) for bothering them with the perversities of modern thought, especially its many forms of idealism. My justification for doing so, however, is that they need to know the extent to which their fellowmen have been misled by academic philosophy in the nineteenth and twentieth centuries.

Returning for the moment to the question of acculturation, to which I made an exception, let me point out that we are all familiar with the commonsense opinion that there is an oriental mind that differs from the occidental mind, or even that the minds of African tribesmen or Australian aborigines are not the same as the minds of European city folk. But this commonsense opinion is not so strong that it cannot be easily made subject to doubt and even to retraction.

With regard to the questions we have been considering, commonsense persons concur in thinking:

1. that the human mind is the same the whole world over, not only in all times and places but also in spite of the diversity of languages and cultures;
2. that there exists a reality that is independent of our minds;

3. that we have minds which enable us to know and understand that reality which, being independent of our minds,
is the *same* reality for all of us, and;

4. that our human experience of that independent reality
has enough in common for all of us that we are able to
talk intelligibly about it to one another.

   In these four statements, the stress is on the sameness of
the human mind everywhere, on the sameness of the reality
that is independent of our minds and the object of its
knowledge, and on what is common or the same in our
experience of it. I will try to defend the central point made
in these four statements.

   Defend it against whom? The answer is: the most eminent figures in modern philosophy and many prominent
professors of philosophy, psychology, linguistics, and cultural anthropology in our contemporary universities. In doing
so, I will be defending common sense against the philosophical mistakes, perplexities, subtleties, and puzzlements that
have arisen in philosophical thought since the end of the
seventeenth century and are widely prevalent today.

   The conflict between philosophy and common sense is
almost entirely modern. Under the educational institutions
of antiquity and the Middle Ages, the great mass of commonsense individuals in the populations were not instructed
by the philosophy that then existed; today, however, with
going to college or university routine for so many and with
current philosophical books available to so many, the situa-
tion is otherwise. The commonsense minds of many are
corrupted and turned against themselves by philosophical
doctrines that urge them to renounce their common sense.

   I have in a recently published book dealt at length with
the philosophical mistakes that are mainly modern.* Here I

---

*See *Ten Philosophical Mistakes* (1985).

wish to comment only on the modern philosophical tendencies that are so subversive of common sense.

Readers would probably be surprised and puzzled to have me say that idealism is a peculiarly modern philosophical malady—puzzled by my use of that word and surprised that there is little or no trace of it in antiquity or in the Middle Ages. The puzzlement comes from a misunderstanding of the word itself. Most people use the word "idealism" to refer to the motivation of those who aspire to go beyond the way things are to the way they ought to be. In this sense, realists are those who acquiesce in the way things are. Idealists are those who wish to improve on them and make them better.

That is not, however, the way I use the word "idealism" or its antonym "realism." My use has nothing at all to do with political, economic, or social reforms or with the betterment of any of our institutions. In that sense, Plato was certainly an idealist in his portrayal of the ideal state in the *Republic*. And even though Plato affirmed the independent existence of ideas as the intelligible objects of the intellect, he was, in that affirmation, a realist because he was asserting the real existence of the ideas—a reality independent of our intellects and the same for all of us.

When I say that idealism is a peculiarly modern philosophical malady, I have in mind a number of theses that have appeared for the first time in modern thought. They are:

1. the denial that there is an independent reality, which is the object of our knowledge and understanding, or at least the denial of a reality that is the same for all of us;

2. the assertion that the structure and features of the world in which we live and the shape of our experience of it are determined by the ideas we employ to think about it;

3. the assertion that the innate structure of our minds—
our senses, our imagination, and our intellect—is itself
constitutive of the world we experience;

4. the belief that the experienced world is not the same as
an unknowable independent reality if that unknowable,
independent reality does in fact exist;

5. the view that there is a variety among our experienced
worlds, varying with the ideas that diverse persons employ in thinking about them;

6. the doctrine that our own ideas are the only objects with
which we can have direct acquaintance, though they can
also somehow be regarded as representations of a reality
with which we cannot have direct acquaintance or of
which we cannot have experience.

In all of these briefly summarized theses, except the first,
the word "idea" is the crucial operative word; hence, the
justification of the epithet "idealism" to describe those who
endorse or espouse one or more of these positions. In the
first statement, the word "idea" does not occur, but a knowable, independent reality is denied, which amounts to saying
that the only objects of our knowledge must either be our
own ideas or an experienced world whose structure and
features are determined by our ideas.

There is something strangely remarkable about the fact
that the idealistic trend in philosophy is predominantly
if not exclusively modern and conspicuously absent in
antiquity and the Middle Ages. The extent of the scientific
knowledge that has come into our possession since the
seventeenth century is incomparably greater than what was
known in all earlier centuries. Yet in the centuries in which
it is generally recognized that knowledge has exploded and
increased many times over, the philosophers have advanced
and embraced doctrines that deny the existence of a reality
that can be known, or they deny that its structure and

features are independent of the minds that claim to know reality.

It almost seems as if the more knowledge we claim to have, knowledge that commonsense individuals acquire and apply, the less philosophers are prepared to accept it as genuine knowledge and the more puzzled they have become about the nature and validity of knowledge.

In earlier chapters I have discussed the materialist strain in modern thought, which resulted in the denial of an intellectual power distinct from and superior to the senses that are embodied in physical organs. Materialism, beginning with Thomas Hobbes, is one of the two main strains in modern thought. The other is idealism, subjective idealism as in Bishop Berkeley or objective idealism as in Immanuel Kant. These two strains are often intermingled, though they may also exist in separation from one another.

These two errors are contrary to one another, which means that both can be false. They involve two fundamental mistakes about the human mind. One is that our own ideas are that which we know, not that whereby we know. The other is the denial of the intellect as a cognitive power quite distinct from the cognitive power of our senses, sensitive memory, and imagination. Only in antiquity and in the Middle Ages are there philosophers who are both realists and, with regard to the intellect, also immaterialists.

The metaphysical materialism that I criticized in the chapters of Part I is opposed to the idealism with which we are going to be concerned in Part II. That idealism denies the existence of an independent reality, material or immaterial. When materialists deny the existence of an immaterial intellect, their doing so derives from their primary dogma: that nothing except bodies or material things really exist. The materialists never question (in fact, they assume or dogmatically assert) that brains really do exist and so do machines.

For the materialists, metaphysics is the first philosophy, but for the idealists it is psychology, especially cognitive psychology. And their interest in that subject is usually limited to epistemology, or the theory of knowledge. We must remember that knowledge may consist of probable truths or truths that have certitude, truths that are beyond the shadow of a doubt.

The Greek word *episteme,* which gives us the root of "epistemology," signifies the latter kind of knowledge, consisting of truths that can be affirmed with certitude. If the search for certainty had been entirely abandoned in modern times, epistemology would never have come into existence. Its prominence, almost its centrality in modern philosophical thought, begins with the German philosopher Immanuel Kant. Whereas for Aristotle metaphysics was the part of speculative philosophy that dealt with the most ultimate questions, for Kant and his followers epistemology replaced metaphysics.

How did this happen? Kant tells us that he was awakened from his dogmatic slumbers as a metaphysician by reading the philosophical works of the Scotsman David Hume. What had Hume done to agitate Kant's mind? Influenced by the mistaken views of his predecessors, Locke and Berkeley, who asserted that ideas were the objects of our experience and that we had immediate acquaintance only with our own ideas, Hume challenged the prevalent acceptance of Newtonian mechanics as knowledge that had certitude.

Horrified by this, Kant developed a theory of the human mind that attributed to it an innate structure that in turn enabled it to determine the structure and features of all possible experience. Kant's theory managed to give the laws of Newtonian mechanics the requisite certitude in the world we experience.

As I have observed elsewhere, Kant could have achieved the same result with much less philosophical effort and ingenuity by simply correcting the errors in Hume's psychology, especially the errors in his philosophy of mind—his denial of the intellect and of abstract ideas, denials that led to a self-refuting nominalism.*

Kant also wished to give certitude to Euclidean geometry, not just as truths about a particular set of mathematical objects (which Hume granted) but as being true, with certitude, about the experienced world. Kant's transcendental forms of intuition saved the truth of Euclid from Hume's skeptical doubts, just as Kant's categories of the understanding saved the certitude of Newtonian mechanics.

The picture of the mind—the senses and the understanding or intellect—that Kant concocted had no corresponding reality. It should have been completely discarded once mathematical and experimental physics overturned Newtonian mechanics as no longer a comprehensive account of the physical universe, and as soon as the non-Euclidean geometries replaced Euclid as applicable to the spherical space of the globe.

That, unfortunately, did not happen. The seeds of Kantian idealism continued to germinate in modern thought and produced philosophical doctrines more and more at variance with the commonsense views that most of us hold, live by, and act on. From the commonsense point of view, some of these post-Kantian doctrines are almost unintelligible in their perversity. Whereas in antiquity and the Middle Ages philosophers merely deepened and extended, by their refinements and reflections, the views of reality and of the experienced world held by men of common sense, philosophers in the last two centuries part company with common sense and move away from it in a diametrically opposed direction.

I said a moment ago that the idealistic tendencies of modern thought are, to put it mildly, at variance with the

*See Ten Philosophical Mistakes, chapter 2 and pp. 193–94.

commonsense views that most of us live by and act on. Our inveterate realism is, perhaps, best illustrated by what goes on in a courtroom when a jury renders a verdict in answer to questions of fact that are being put on trial. Our business transactions as well as our freedom from fines and imprisonment, even death in capital cases, depend on our acceptance of a jury's verdict that certain things are true or false with sufficient probability to be relied upon.

In the world of real existences, the jury's verdict is that this probably did happen and that probably did not. We accept without question that there is a reality to be known with probability, not certitude. We also accept without question that the testimony that reports the experience of witnesses enables us to know with sufficient probability what really happened.

What I have just said about the conduct of a jury trial applies to almost all the commercial transactions in which we engage. The questions to be resolved in such transactions are almost always questions about what really is or is not the case.

When philosophers are puzzled by what commonsense persons claim to know and that they act on such knowledge, that philosophical puzzlement in no way alters what is known. All sorts of perplexities arise in philosophical attempts to explain how we know something and how we assess the validity of our claim to know or the probability of our knowledge. But these perplexities and puzzlements, even if they are so profound as to be irresolvable, do not invalidate our claim to know something or alter our assessment of the probability of that knowledge.

It is a peculiarly modern error to suppose that because we cannot give a completely acceptable account of how we know something, we therefore do not in fact know it. The twentieth-century philosopher Ludwig Wittgenstein said that philosophy is doing the work it should do when it unties the knots in our understanding, when it overcomes the difficulties encountered in explaining how we know something. But, in my view, most of those knots and difficulties result from the errors of philosophers who tied the knots in the first place. Hence, it seems to me that it would be better to correct the original errors rather than work at untying the knots that resulted from those errors.

For example, commonsense persons have no doubt whatsoever that other human beings have minds so much like their own that no insuperable obstacles to communication are encountered. It may be difficult to give an adequate analytical account of how we know this, since the minds of other persons are not directly observable by us, and reasons must be given to validate the inference to the conclusion that others do in fact really have minds like our own. But however extensive and subtle that philosophical account may become, our commonsense inference from observable evidence available to us remains sound and supports the conclusion we act on without doubt.

Nor do commonsense persons need the prodding of philosophers to acknowledge that reality is not always what it appears to be. In jewelry stores all of us have questioned whether the gem being displayed is a real pearl or an imitation, a real diamond or a fake. When we say "it looks like a diamond, but . . ." we are making a distinction between appearance and reality. That commonsense distinction may require philosophical refinement in order to assess the difference between reality in itself and quite apart from us, and reality as we experience it. But philosophy goes astray when in modern times its idealist tendency leads it to deny that reality in itself and apart from us exists and is knowable, or to deny that our experience of reality gives rise to knowledge about it.

To deny a reality independent of our mind is to deny that anything ever existed before man came on this earth.

Yet our paleontologists and our zoologists tell us what that reality was like before man existed. To say that reality before mankind existed is unknowable is to deny all our scientific knowledge of the prehuman world.*

All of this is so preposterous and perverse that it will be hard for commonsense readers to take it seriously. Nevertheless, those readers must be told and must believe that there is hardly any doctrine so weird and crackpot that philosophers, especially modern philosophers, have not seriously espoused it.

*Professor Etienne Gilson, the eminent French philosopher and historian of philosophy, has written a book that recounts the rise of philosophical idealism in modern times, in its first phase beginning with Descartes and its second phase beginning with Kant. The book also contains a vigorous defense of the philosophical realism that preceded it in antiquity and in the Middle Ages; and argues for its restoration today. See *Methodical Realism* (1990), pp. 11, 21, 56, 81, 91, 102, and especially chapter 5.

CHAPTER 8

About What Exists Independently of the Mind

(INCLUDING A NOTE ABOUT REALITY IN RELATION TO QUANTUM MECHANICS)

WHAT IS NONMIND in the universe—that which lies totally outside the mind and would exist if the universe contained no minds and would be exactly the same in character whether or not thinking and knowing existed?

What shall we call the totality of existence that is external to the mind? The obvious name for it is reality but, as we shall see, to call it that requires a number of cautionary qualifications.

Are we considering mind in general, any and all minds, or are we considering your mind and mine? Only if we are considering mind in general does the word "reality" signify everything in existence that is nonmind. But if I am considering my own mind, then what is external to it includes your mind, all other human minds, the minds of animals, and possibly the mind of God.

For you as for me, whatever other minds there are belong to the realm of real existences—things whose existence does not depend upon the existence of my mind or upon its operations. My mind is part of reality for you, as your mind is part of reality for me.

What is external to my mind not only includes other minds but also my body. That certainly is the case if there is truth in the view advanced in chapter 4 that the intellectual human mind cannot be reductively identified with the brain as an organ of the human body. But even in the extreme materialist view that identifies the actions of the mind with the actions of the brain, it still remains a fact that the activities of all organs or components of the body that are not operations of the brain and nervous system belong to reality—the realm that is not mind.

Two criteria enter into the definition of the realm that can properly be called reality. One is its existence independent of the human mind in general. The cosmos that physical science describes as beginning its present career, not its creation, with the big bang fifteen or eighteen billion years ago, or this planet in our solar system to which scientists attribute an antiquity that long antedates the first appearance of the human species, fulfills this first criterion.

To deny that the cosmos or this planet is independent of the human mind, which claims to have verifiable knowledge of it, is to deny that claim; for if the existence of the cosmos and this earth were dependent on the existence of the human mind, then the great antiquity that scientists attribute to them must be false. If their existence is dependent on the human mind, then their age is no greater than that of the species *Homo sapiens*.

The second criterion is independence in structure and character as well as in existence. Reality is not only that which exists whether we are present to think about it or not; it is also that which is determinately whatever it is—has the structure and character that it has—no matter how we think about it. Our thinking about it, our efforts to attain knowledge of it, has no constitutive effect upon it. Quantum mechanics, in which we attempt to measure the position and velocity of subatomic particles, would appear to be an exception to this statement. I will return to this point later in a note appended at the end of this chapter.

The appearance of the species *Homo sapiens* on earth added to the constituents of the reality that preexisted man's origin, but that addition did not change the character of any of the other components of reality. They did, indeed, become objects of human knowledge, which they were not before man the knower came into existence. Becoming an object of knowledge does not change the character of that which is known. If it did, knowledge would be impossible. For us to know something, the character it has as *knowable* must be the character it has *as known*.

The realm of mind includes much that does not belong to the realm of real existence as defined by the two criteria we have just considered. For each of us it includes, first of all, everything we properly regard as subjective, as something each of us experiences that is entirely private and open to inspection by no one else: all of our bodily feelings, our aches and pains, our pleasures, our fear and anger, our desires.

Please note that in the foregoing enumeration of the subjective elements in human experience, I have not mentioned anything that functions cognitively in the minimum sense that it refers to something beyond itself that is its object. Thus, for example, a memory refers to some past event that is its object; a percept refers to some present thing or happening that is its object; a concept refers to something that is an object of thought.

At this point, readers are called upon to remember what was said in chapter 2. Such mental components as memories, percepts, and concepts are not themselves subjectively experienceable by us in the same way that each of us experiences his own bodily feelings, emotions, and desires. Memories, percepts, and concepts exist in our minds solely to perform the function of presenting us with objects remembered, objects perceived, and objects of thought. Through them, we are conscious of their objects, but we are never conscious or aware of them.

Philosophers in the past distinguished between two realms of being, calling one the realm of *entia reale,* and the other the realm of *entia rationis.* The first of these we have already described as that which exists independently of the human mind and has a determinate character that does not depend on how we think about it, the realm of real existence. In sharp contrast, the realm of *entia rationis* consists of those things that have existence only in this individual mind or that one. It consists also of those fictions of thought or conceptual constructs that exist in the minds of scientists or philosophers, as well as the purely subjective elements of our private, personal experience. Their existence is as completely dependent on the existence of my mind or yours as the existence of *entia reale* is totally independent of the existence of my mind or yours, and of the human mind in general.

This twofold division of the realms of being leaves a third realm to be accounted for, one that stands between two extremes. At one extreme, we have the realm the components of which have real existence. At the other extreme, we have the realm the components of which exist only in the mind. The middle ground between these two is occupied by the objects of our perceptions, of our memories, and of our thoughts. While these objects are not independent of the human mind in general, they are independent of one or another individual human mind.

Anything that you and I and other persons can discuss as an object that is common to our experience belongs in this middle realm. Here is the perceived object that you and I are discussing when we hold a bottle of wine in our hands. Here is the remembered occasion you and I are discussing when we talk about a wedding we recently attended. Here is the conceived mathematical infinity that you and I are discussing when we argue about that object of thought.

If there were no perceptions, memories, and conceptions, these commonly perceived, remembered, and thought about objects would not exist. But they do not exist only for my mind or for yours, as my toothache exists only in mine, and your feeling of anger exists only in yours. For example, three persons could have been discussing that perceived bottle of wine, and two of them could continue discussing it if one of them walked away. If I were the one who walked away, that perceived object would not have ceased to exist. Its existence did not depend upon my mind. The same is true of the remembered wedding discussed by three or the mathematical infinity argued about by three. The object being considered would not cease to exist with the disappearance of any one of the three.

There is a reason for complicating the picture by adding this intermediate realm between the real (that which is independent of mind in general) and the subjective (that which is dependent exclusively on my mind or yours). The middle ground, you will remember, is occupied by objects that, while not dependent exclusively on my mind or yours, are dependent for their existence on mind in general and would not exist if there were no human minds at all.

Now we must draw a line that divides these objects into two groups. On the one hand are objects validly perceived or remembered that really exist or that once existed in the past, though they may no longer exist at present. On the other hand are all conceived objects, or objects of thought, that are radically different from perceived and remembered objects.

Unlike the latter, which have real existence as well as objective existence, objects of thought may or may not have real existence in addition to having objective existence. They may be simply *entia rationis*—fictions or constructions of the mind. Does the conceived object really exist is a question we must ask about any object of thought, a question that we may be able to answer affirmatively in some cases and not in others.

That question should never be asked about a validly perceived or remembered object, yet in modern philosophy, and only in modern philosophy, it has been asked persistently. In antiquity and the Middle Ages, no philosopher ever asked for a proof, or anything like a proof, for the reality of the external world, for the reality of the past, or for the reality of other minds.

There were, of course, skeptics in antiquity, but their skepticism in its most extreme form focused on truth. They asserted that no statement that could be made was either true or false, failing to acknowledge that their own assertion, taken as either true or false, led to self-refutation.

Not until Descartes in the seventeenth century did any philosopher engage in an experiment of doubt that required him to argue for the existence of the external physical world. Doubting the evidence presented by his sense, Descartes took refuge in what appeared to him an undeniable truth. His doubting involved his thinking, and if he was thinking, he could not avoid the conclusion that a thinking being existed.

However, his *Cogito, ergo sum* (I think, therefore I am) did not establish the existence of Descartes, the human individual, body and mind, but only the existence of his intellect, the agency of his doubting and thinking. From that conclusion, he developed a highly questionable argument for the existence of God, a perfect being who, being morally as well as ontologically perfect, would not deceive him. With that conviction established, Descartes declared himself willing to trust his sense-perceptions—of his own body and other bodies—and so finally no longer hesitated to affirm the existence of physical reality, the realm of bodies in motion.

Since Descartes, there have been many other attempts to prove what needs no proof, as well as denials of what cannot be denied—physical reality. To say that its existence is evident to our senses is correct, but that correct statement requires a brief explication.

When you or I say that we *perceive* something—a moving vehicle that we see or hear—we are, in effect, asserting the existence of the perceived object. The statement "I perceive X" is inseparable from the assertion "X exists." If X did not exist, it would be imperceptible, and the statement "I perceive X" would be false. In its place, there should be a true statement about me—namely, "he is hallucinating X."

If I am not alone in perceiving X, I can be relatively certain that I am perceiving, not hallucinating, and that X, the perceived object, exists. If I am hallucinating, not perceiving, I will be alone in claiming to perceive X (e.g., a pink elephant in my hospital room). While under the influence of whatever it is that causes my hallucination, I am not likely to be persuaded that it is not there, that I am not perceiving it.

This can be summed up by simply reversing the maxim of Bishop Berkeley's subjective idealism: *esse est percipi* (to be is to be perceived). The implication that nothing exists unless it is perceptible and also perceived runs counter to facts so obvious that Berkeley's maxim is readily seen to be false. But the reverse is true: *percipi est esse* (whatever is perceived really exists).*

As for the reality of the past, a simple inference that any reasonable person would make suffices for its affirmation. I have become acquainted with John Dokes in the present. What I know about human procreation and the succession of generations allows me to believe without hesitation that John Dokes had a father, a grandfather, and a great-grandfather, and so on back to the prerevolutionary period when his ancestors first came to this country. He may, of course, be telling me fibs about his forebears, but it is at least a reasonable inference from his perceived existence to the conclusion that he had ancestors in a remote past that really existed many years ago and no longer exist today.

Finally, we come to the question about the real existence of minds other than our own. Here, once again, there is no need for subtle arguments or attempts to prove what does not require proof. The simple fact of ordinary conversation between human beings, involving questions and answers about matters of their common experiences, suffices for the conviction that each of them has a human mind, one not essentially different from the other.

If I am one of the two persons and you the other, I hear in what you say evidence that the same kind of mental activity occurring in me is also occurring in you. If I am a third person listening to a conversation between two others, my understanding of the interchanges that I hear imputes to the speakers' mental activity of the same kind that I am experiencing myself.

We noted earlier that there are two criteria, not one, that enter into the definition of a reality external to the human

*To affirm the existence of imperceptible conceptual objects, their existence, according to William of Ockham, a medieval philosopher of science, must be needed to explain observed phenomena. The fallacy of reification consists in their affirmation without the need to do so.

mind and that is genuinely knowable by it. The first is its independent existence. The second is the independence of its structure and character. Neither in its existence nor in its character does reality depend upon the existence of the human mind or upon the activity of the human mind in its processes of thinking, believing, and knowing. If this were not the case, truth would have a queer meaning, if anything at all deserved to be called truth.

We may think truly or falsely; we may harbor true or false beliefs, but false knowledge is a contradiction in terms. If I claim to know something, my claim amounts to asserting that I have in my mind the truth about it. I may grasp that truth with certitude or with some shadow of a doubt, but if my claim is false, then I do not have knowledge. Hence, whatever conditions make my assertion true also support my claim to having certain or probable knowledge. Truth and knowledge are inseparable.

In the history of Western thought, there are only two major theories of truth, each with minor variations. One is the correspondence theory of truth; the other, the coherence theory of truth.

The correspondence theory asserts (1) that there is a reality independent of the mind, and (2) that truth (or, what is the same thing, knowledge) exists in the mind when the mind agrees with, conforms or corresponds to, that independent reality. When what I assert agrees with the way things really are, my assertions are true; otherwise they are false.

The correspondence theory of truth includes the coherence theory as a subordinate aspect of itself. If, in my thinking about an independent reality, I make assertions that are inconsistent with one another to the extent that both cannot be true, though both may be false, that incoherence is a sign of some failure in my thinking to correspond with reality. The principle of noncontradiction is both an ontological principle (the principle that contradictories cannot coexist in reality) as well as a logical rule (the rule that thinking cannot be correct if it is self-contradictory).

The conflict between the two theories occurs only when exponents of the coherence criterion of truth deny the correspondence criterion. They claim that *nothing but* perfect coherence in our thought, the absence of all inconsistencies and contradictions, assures us that we have the truth in our mind.

What underlies the denial of the correspondence criterion of truth? Only one thing: the denial of an independent reality that is knowable. Immanuel Kant did not deny a reality independent of the mind, but that reality—*dinge an sich* (things in themselves)—he also declared completely unknowable.

In Kant's view, the realm of objective and public experience that is knowable by us is shaped and determined in its characteristics by the innate structure of the human mind. Accordingly, there is no point in talking about correspondence or agreement between what is in the human mind and what is itself a product of the human mind. Though Kant himself did not appeal to the coherence theory of truth, the absolute idealists in Germany and England, who followed in his wake, did.

In the first decades of this century, there was great agitation in the philosophical journals about the theory of truth. At the center of this controversy were many essays written by the English idealist F. H. Bradley at Oxford and by the American pragmatist William James at Harvard. Bradley attacked James's theory of truth without distinguishing between (1) what for James was a correspondence theory of truth in general and (2) what for James was a pragmatic test whereby we can tell whether a particular thought or proposition is true.

James expounded that pragmatic test as follows. If our

thinking leads us to successful results in action (if, in other words, our thinking works out well in practice), we have a hold on truth. Our thinking would fail to work well, it would not lead to a successful result, if it did not correspond with a reality independent of our minds.

He criticized Bradley's coherence theory of truth, not as entirely incorrect but as radically insufficient.* Its insufficiency is attested by the fact that persons in hospitals for the insane, suffering delusions of grandeur or persecution, manage to develop thoroughly coherent and completely consistent accounts to support the delusion that they are Napoleon in exile or the victim of a political conspiracy.

Let us for the moment suppose that the only correct theory of truth is the correspondence theory. Let us consider that theory as including a subordinate criterion of coherence or consistency, and also as supporting the application of the pragmatic test for telling whether a particular thought or statement is in fact true or false. Let us add to this pragmatic test other empirical tests of verifiability or falsifiability.

Let us further acknowledge that all such tests presuppose the main tenet of the correspondence theory of truth—namely, that the structure and character of reality is independent of the human mind. Finally, let us recognize that the correspondence theory of truth and the pragmatic test for discerning whether something is true or false conform to the commonsense view of the matter.

What shall we say of those modern European thinkers

---

*Bradley mistakenly took the pragmatic test of truth as if it were a definition of what constitutes truth in general. Here is an example of how the pragmatic test works: two men in a canoe floating downstream underestimate the distance of a life-threatening cataract. Thinking it four miles farther downstream, when in fact it is only two miles away, they doze off and suffer the disaster that results from their misjudgment. The pragmatic test is not a definition of what constitutes truth in general, but it presupposes that definition in the correspondence theory of truth.

before and after Kant who espouse idealism, or of those contemporary American philosophers who, claiming they are not idealists, nevertheless deny that reality has a structure and character independent of the human mind?

For idealists, there is no reality independent of mind. For those who are not idealists, a reality may exist without dependence on the mind, but its structure and character are not independent of the mind. In either case, must we not say that they have no grounds, or at least no adequate grounds, for testing and affirming truths?

As a consequence, must we not also say that they cannot regard scientific investigation or philosophical inquiry as efforts to attain knowledge of reality? Knowledge of the human mind and of its actions and effects, perhaps; but not knowledge of a reality that is unaffected by the mind's activities.

It may not come as a surprise to some of my readers, especially those who have acquaintance with the history of modern thought, that post-Kantian idealism in eighteenth- and nineteenth-century Germany and England dominated the philosophical scene.* But many readers will probably be surprised to learn that there has been quite recently a revival of the idealist error by contemporary philosophers in America.

They have attributed to the human mind constructive, formative, and creative powers that, in effect, nullify its cognitive power—its power to attain knowledge and to ascertain truths in the light of empirical evidence. This is all the more remarkable in view of the fact that, at the beginning of this century, in its first two decades, philosophers, working in teams, effectively criticized and attempted to refute the then regnant idealism.

---

*Readers may remember from chapter 7 that idealism—the opposite of commonsense realism—is a peculiarly modern error, both before and after Kant.

In 1912, six philosophers cooperatively produced a book entitled *The New Realism*.* In an appendix, each wrote a summary of his position. Both Professor Edwin Holt and Professor Walter Marvin stressed their common view that objects of knowledge are not conditioned or affected by their being known. "Realism," wrote Professor William Montague, "is opposed to subjectivism or epistemological idealism, which denies that things can exist apart from an experience of them, or independently of the cognitive relation." Professor Walter Pitkin reiterated this by saying that "the realist holds that things known are not products of the knowing relation nor essentially dependent for their existence or behavior on that relation."

In 1921, seven philosophers published what they called a cooperative study of the problem of knowledge, entitled *Essays in Critical Realism*.† In that volume, Professor George Santayana's essay set forth three proofs of realism and concluded with the following statement:

> You cannot prove realism to a complete skeptic or idealist, but you can show an honest man that he is not a complete skeptic or idealist, but a realist at heart. So long as he is alive his sincere philosophy must fulfill the assumptions of his life and not destroy them.

Not only Santayana but all the rest of the writers in these two volumes repeatedly pointed out the conflict between idealism and common sense. The commonsense view of a

---

*Edwin B. Holt, Walter T. Marvin, William Pepperrell Montague, Ralph Barton Perry, Walter B. Pitkin, and Edward Gleason Spaulding. In England, at about the same time, G. E. Moore wrote an essay entitled "The Refutation of Idealism," in *Philosophical Studies* (1922).

†Durant Drake, Arthur O. Lovejoy, James Bissett Pratt, Arthur K. Rogers, George Santayana, Roy Wood Sellars, and C. A. Strong. I call attention especially to pp. 87–97 of the essay by Professor Pratt, in which readers will find a brief and extremely clear account of the philosophical errors in modern thought that, both prior to and after Kant, gave rise to idealism in its many forms.

reality independent of the mind, which permits the mind to have a cognitive relation to it, is that of realism.

Early in the twentieth century, Jacques Maritain distinguished sharply between (a) empiriometric science, for which the only reality is that which can be measured and for which the measurements made can be fed into powerful mathematical equations, and (b) the metaphysical knowledge of aspects of reality that exist, though they are beyond the possibility of measurement.* He called attention to the fact that the great physicists of the twentieth century, from Einstein on, allowed themselves to slip from saying "what is not measurable *by* a physicist has no reality *for* a physicist" (which is true) into saying "what is not measurable has no existence in reality" (which is just as plainly false).

Forty and fifty years later, after the publication in 1962 of Thomas K. Kuhn's book *The Structure of Scientific Revolutions,* natural scientists and philosophers of science at the Institute for Advanced Study in Princeton argued with one another about whether science was making progress in getting at the truth about reality.

Were not successive scientific hypotheses or theories like different pairs of glasses having different tints through which nature might be viewed, each an alternative view of the way things are? Did we have grounds for being assured that, in this succession of regnant theories, science was getting nearer and nearer to the ultimate truth about the cosmos?

---

*I would like to refer readers to pertinent passages in a book by Maritain, the translation of which I edited: *Scholasticism and Politics* (1940), chapter 11, on science and philosophy, especially pp. 28, 30–34, 37–38. See also his *The Degrees of Knowledge* (1938). Here Maritain espouses the critical realism of Aristotle and Aquinas, a realism that antedates by many centuries the modern forms of idealism. It is not in any way an attempt to refute these modern errors as, for example, is G. E. Moore's "The Refutation of Idealism," first published in *Mind* in 1903 and issued in a collection of his essays published in 1922 under the title *Philosophical Studies.* More recently, the Gifford Lectures in 1974–76 by Stanley Jaki, *The Road of Science and the Ways to God,* contain another refutation of idealism. See chapter 9, "The Illusions of Idealism."

Professor Kuhn raised the question whether it really helps to imagine that there is one full, objective, true account of nature and that the proper measure of scientific achievement is the extent to which it brings us nearer to that ultimate goal. Kuhn doubted it, but another philosopher of science, Dudley Shapero, who came to the Institute for Advanced Study in the late 1970s, disagreed with Kuhn. He denied that seeing through glasses of one or another tint makes a true understanding of nature impossible. The glasses we wear may color our view of reality, but surely they do not constitute its structure or character. In a review of Kuhn's book, Shapero described it as "a sustained attack on the prevailing image of scientific change as a linear process of ever-increasing knowledge."

Even more recently, contemporary American philosophers and psychologists, such as Nelson Goodman, Jerome Bruner, and Richard Rorty, have published books that revive the Kantian retreat from an independent reality and give us a new form of idealism that Professor Bruner calls a "constructivist philosophy."*

In his review of Goodman's *Of Mind and Other Matters*, Bruner makes clear that constructivism, "contrary to common sense," holds that "there is no unique 'real world' that preexists and is independent of human mental activity." Subsequently in the review, Bruner explains that "the constructivist view that what exists is a product of what is thought, was first worked out by Kant." But unlike Kant, "Goodman refuses to assign any privileged status or any 'ultimate reality to any particular world that we may create.'" And "once we give up the idea of an aboriginal reality," Bruner writes, "we lose the criterion of correspondence between statement or hypothesis and 'reality' as a

---

*Professor Bruner's book is entitled *Actual Minds, Possible Worlds* (1986). Professor Goodman wrote *Ways of World-Making* (1978) as well as *Of Mind and Other Matters* (1984); Professor Rorty's book is *Philosophy and the Mirror of Nature* (1979).

way of distinguishing between true and false models of the world."*

REALITY IN RELATION TO QUANTUM MECHANICS

Earlier in this chapter I promised to return to the apparent conflict between twentieth-century quantum mechanics and the realist's affirmation of an independent reality, independent not only in its existence but also in its determinate structure and character. The conflict first arose from Heisenberg's principle of uncertainty, which has also been called the principle of indeterminacy.

In subatomic physics, the velocity of the electron's motion within the atom and its spatial position at the same time cannot both be measured with complete accuracy. The measuring process itself so affects the electron being measured that it prevents us from ascertaining, at the same time, both velocity and position with exactitude. In addition, according to the special character of the experimental measurement, the electron is either a wave or it is a particle. As one shifts from one mode of experimentation to another, the electron appears to change its character.

The question then arises whether the indeterminacy exists in reality or should be regarded instead as indeterminability by us—an unavoidable limitation upon our knowledge of reality rather than a feature of reality itself. Almost all quantum physicists are firmly committed to the position that the indeterminacy exists in reality. If that is the case, then reality is not determinate in all respects. It is false to say that the electron has, at a given time, a determinate position and velocity, even though we cannot exactly determine both at the same time.†

*New York Review of Books, March 27, 1986, pp. 46–49.
†See Werner Heisenberg's Physics and Philosophy (1958), chapter 10, on language and reality in modern physics.

The underlying thesis that I am espousing runs counter to the position taken by most physicists. It is that the aspects of reality measurable by physicists are not all the aspects of reality that exist. Most physicists, on the contrary, appear to espouse the opposite thesis, that what they cannot measure does not really exist.

Take, for example, the statement by Professor N. David Mermin, a theoretical physicist, that "clocks do not measure some preexisting thing called 'time,' but that our concept of time is simply a convenient way to abstract the common behavior of all those things we call 'clocks.'" It is this view of time that, in the general theory of relativity, led Einstein to deny the existence of simultaneity between events at remote points in space. He converted the immeasurability of simultaneity into its nonexistence in reality.

Stephen Hawking, in his recent book *A Brief History of Time,* goes even further in the same direction. He quite explicitly espouses the thesis that what is not measurable by physicists does not really exist. Physicists cannot measure time before the big bang; therefore, it did not exist in reality. Physicists cannot measure time after the cosmos freezes up in the ultimate singularity of a black hole; therefore, time will come to an end. The correct title for Hawking's book should have been *A Brief History of Measurable Time.* The book is not about time as the philosopher understands it, much of which may be immeasurable.

Paradoxically, both Einstein and Hawking would appear to be involved in contradicting themselves. The same Einstein who denies simultaneity between remote events in space because of our inability to measure them also argues, against other physicists, that our inability to accurately measure the velocity and position of the electron does not mean that at a given moment in time the electron does not occupy a determinate position and does not have a determinate velocity.*

The same Hawking who, in his recent book, proceeds on the assumption that what is not measurable by physicists does not have any existence in reality also does not hesitate to refer to God and God's mind as if both had reality even though neither is measurable by physicists.

What is measurable by physicists are only certain partial aspects of reality; other aspects of reality exist even if they are not measurable by physicists. In addition, I think it can be argued cogently that our commonsense view of reality and the philosophical exposition of that view deals with aspects of reality more fundamental than the measurable aspects treated by physicists.†

I think the matter can be further clarified by the following considerations. In the first place, let us note Bohr's principle of complementarity, which said that conceiving the electron as a wave and conceiving it as a particle were not only alternative ways of conceiving it, but also complementary ways of doing so. As Heisenberg pointed out, these are "two complementary descriptions of the same reality. Any of these descriptions can be only partially true; these must be limitations to the use of the particle concept as well as of the wave concept, else one could not avoid contradictions. If one takes into account those limitations, which can be expressed by the uncertainty relations, the contradictions disappear."‡ In other words, Bohr's principle affirms the

---

*For a revealing account of conflicting tendencies in the mind and in the thinking of Albert Einstein, see Stanley Jaki's *Angels, Apes, and Men* (1984), pp. 90–97; and for a penetrating critique of the mistake of attributing indeterminacy in reality to what is only indeterminability (or immeasurability) in quantum mechanics, see Jaki's Gifford lectures, *The Road of Science and the Ways to God*, chapters 11–14.

†I have presented that argument in another book; see chapter 10 of *Ten Philosophical Mistakes* (1985).

‡Werner Heisenberg, *Physics and Philosophy: The Revolution in Modern Science* (1958), p. 43.

principle of noncontradiction as governing our thought, and it is a correct rule of thought only if noncontradiction is an ontological principle also governing reality.*

In the second place, let us observe the extraordinary difference between experimental measurements performed by scientists in the realm of classical or macroscopic physics— the realm of all objects larger than the atom. Here the properties of the object being measured by the physicists are properties inherent in the objects themselves and would exist in reality as such whether measured by physicists or not. In other words, the physical properties of the object and the object itself are not in any way affected by the scientific measurement of them.†

The difference between quantum theory and classical physics lies in the fact that when we try to measure what is happening *inside* the atom (and thus are dealing with objects smaller than the atom), our experimental measurements are intrusive, affect the object being studied, and confer upon the subatomic entities or events the properties attributed to them. Unlike the supra-atomic physical objects or events, these subatomic objects or events do not have in themselves well-defined intrinsic properties. Their properties are conferred upon them by the experimental measurements made by the quantum physicists.

The crucial problem to be solved, which Einstein tried but failed to solve, can be formulated by two alternative questions as follows: (1) Is the physical reality of objects

---

*In this same book, Heisenberg also points out that "this again emphasizes the subjective element in the description of atomic events, since the measuring device has been constructed by the observer, and we have to remember that what we observe is not nature itself, but nature exposed to our method of questioning . . . [and our] trying to get an answer from experiment by the means at our disposal" (p. 58).

†For example, the measurements in the research that resulted in the Table of Atomic Weights did *not* confer on the atoms the weights assigned to them. They were properties inherent in the atoms weighed.

and events within the interior of the atom in itself determinate in character? (2) Is reality at the level of subatomic objects and events indeterminate in itself? If the first question is answered affirmatively, then Einstein was right in maintaining that quantum theory is an incomplete account of subatomic reality.

The question was not answered satisfactorily by the thought experiment called the "Einstein-Podolsky-Rosen Paradox." The later thinking and experimental work that led to the confirmation of the Bell theorem favors the second answer. Almost all quantum physicists today accept the answer as correct. They think they *know* that subatomic reality, unlike supra-atomic reality, is indeterminate in character. The indeterminacy attributed to subatomic objects and events by Heisenberg's uncertainty principles is not just their indeterminability *by us;* it is intrinsic to subatomic reality.

Many quantum physicists are quite content to embrace the paradox that supra-atomic and subatomic reality are strikingly different in character—the one intrinsically determinate in character, the other intrinsically indeterminate. But from a philosophical point of view, that difference between supra-atomic and subatomic reality—both in their different intrinsic characters, independent of the human mind—is a mystery that calls for further thought. It is just possible that quantum physicists may not be correct in their present view of the matter.

The two questions to which the quantum physicists think they know the right answers are philosophical, not scientific questions—questions which, if they can be answered at all, can be answered only by thought, not by research. Unfortunately, for it has an effect on twentieth-century thought, the quantum physicists presume to answer the questions *as if* the questions were answerable only by them in the light of their research findings. That is a serious mistake on their part. It is an egregious example of the presumption that scientists in many fields have frequently made in the twentieth century.

A brief history of the atom may help us to do the philosophical thinking that is called for. Atomic theory began in the sixth century B.C. with the physical speculations of Democritus and Leucippus. The atom was then thought to be a solid and indivisible particle of matter, with no interior. That conception of the atom was espoused by such sixteenth- and seventeenth-century physicists as Galileo and Newton, and by such seventeenth- and eighteenth-century philosophers as Hobbes and Locke.

In all these centuries, from antiquity down to the first half of the nineteenth century, the atom, thus conceived, was regarded as belonging to the realm of *entia rationis,* not to the realm of *entia reale:* that is, it was regarded as a scientific fiction or theoretical construct, the real existence of which had not been experimentally established. Only in the first years of the twentieth century did the experimental work on atomic radiation establish two physical facts: *one,* that atoms had real physical existence; and *two,* that they were not solid particles of matter but had discrete interior constituents. This led a little later to the hypothesis that they might even be divisible.

During all this time, the interior of the atom was not explored by intrusive measuring devices. That occurred later in the twentieth century and led to the first atomic fission in the 1940s. Quantum mechanics—the experimental and theoretical study of the interior structure of the atom—became the great revolution in twentieth-century physics, presenting us with the mysterious difference between subatomic and supra-atomic reality. That, philosophically, is more revolutionary than quantum mechanics itself.

Atoms existed in the centuries preceding the scientific work that established their real existence. Atoms had interiors, in which physical entities existed and physical events occurred, in all the centuries before it was scientifically established that atoms had interiors in which subatomic entities existed and subatomic events occurred. It is certainly fair to ask what the subatomic physical reality was like in all those centuries. Was it like the subatomic reality described by twentieth-century quantum theory? Was it a physical reality having the intrinsic character of indeterminacy, or was it an intrinsically determinate physical reality like the supra-atomic reality of classical physics?

To answer that question philosophically, it is necessary to bear in mind one point that the quantum physicists appear to forget or overlook. At the same time that the Heisenberg uncertainty principles were established, quantum physicists acknowledged that the intrusive experimental measurements that provided the data used in the mathematical formulations of quantum theory *conferred on subatomic objects and events that indeterminate character.*

The foregoing intalicized words imply that the indeterminate character of subatomic objects and events is *not* intrinsic to them—*not* properties they have quite apart from their being affected in any way by the measurements made by intrusive experimental devices.

If the cause of the indeterminacy attributed to the sub-atomic objects and events by quantum theory is the intrusive and disturbing measurement of those objects and events, which confers upon them properties (namely, intrinsic indeterminacy) not possessed by supra-atomic physical objects and events, then *does not elimination of the cause also eliminate the effect?*

Philosophically speaking, the answer to that question must be affirmative. The opposite answer, given by the quantum theorists, *as if* they knew it to be the right answer as a result of their scientific research, cannot draw any support from the fact that their theory, which is based on their own intrusive measurements, gives rise to completely verifiable predictions.

If the cause of indeterminacy attributed to subatomic objects and events in quantum theory is the intrusive and disturbing measurement of those objects and events that confers upon them properties that supra-atomic physical objects and events do not possess, then does not the elimination of that cause also eliminate its effect?

In other words, was not the physical reality of subatomic objects not different from but like the physical reality of supra-atomic events, in all those earlier centuries when the atom existed and had an interior that the experimental measurements of quantum mechanics did not intrude upon and disturb?

The following imaginary example may help us to understand the philosophical answer to the questions posed. Imagine a pool of water in a hermetically sealed house that has endured for centuries with no human beings ever inside it. During all that time, the character of the water in the pool is completely placid. Then suddenly human beings find the house and find a way of opening it up to outside influences such as winds; and, in addition, they enter the house and jump into the pool without first looking at the surface of the water. The water in the pool affected by outside influences *and especially* by the humans jumping into the pool is disturbed and no longer has the character of complete placidity. The humans describe the pool as it appeared to them after they jumped into it and attribute wave motions and other properties to it.

Can quantum mechanics, through its experimentally performed measurements, be a disturbing and intrusive influence that affects the character of subatomic reality, and at the same time, can its exponents be certain that subatomic reality has the intrinsic indeterminacy that quantum theory attributes to it? Is the *unexamined* interior of the atom intrinsically indeterminate in character, or is it like the determinate character of supra-atomic reality?

God knows the answer, as Einstein at the beginning of his controversy with Bohr declared when he said that God does not throw dice, which implied that the *unexamined* subatomic reality is as determinate as a supra-atomic reality.

Whether or not God knows the answer, experimental science *does not know it.* Nor does philosophy know it with certitude. But philosophy can give a good reason for favoring the answer that affirms similitude between the character of subatomic and of supra-atomic reality—both intrinsically determinate. The reason is that quantum theorists repeatedly acknowledge their intrusive and disturbing measurements are the cause of the indeterminacy they attribute to subatomic objects and events. It follows, therefore, that indeterminacy cannot be intrinsic to subatomic reality.

Unfortunately, in this century, quantum theory has inadvertently given undue comfort to the worst tendency in contemporary thought—its philosophical idealism or constructivism, which denies a reality that exists completely independent of the human mind and has whatever intrinsic character it has without being affected by how the human mind knows it or thinks about it.*

To sum up: the quantum theory is a theory of the examined interior of the atom. The scientific examination of that interior is, according to quantum theory, an intrusive disturbance of what is going on there. It follows that further developments of quantum theory and additional scientific investigation cannot tell us about the character of the unexamined atomic interior.

---

*The great English mathematician G. H. Hardy has a comment on this worth quoting: "It may be that modern physics fits best into some framework of idealistic philosophy. I do not believe it, but there are some eminent physicists who say so. Pure mathematics, on the other hand, seems to me a rock on which all idealism founders: 317 is a prime, not because we think so, or because our minds are shaped in one way rather than another, but *because it is so,* because mathematical reality is built that way." G. H. Hardy, *A Mathematician's Apology* (1940), p. 130.

Einstein was right that the quantum theory is an incomplete account of subatomic reality, but he was wrong in thinking that that incompleteness could be remedied by any means at the disposal of science. Why? Because the question that quantum theory and subatomic research cannot answer is a question for philosophy, not science.

CHAPTER 9

About What the Mind
Draws from Experience

THE REALITY that is independent of the human mind, without the existence of which knowledge and truth would be impossible, is one and the same reality for all human beings.

Experience is not independent of the human mind. If it were, we would not speak of it as human experience. To speak of reality as human is to violate an essential feature of it: its independence of the human mind. But while human experience is mind-dependent as reality is not, it is also, to a considerable extent, the same for all human beings. The reason why there is a common core in human experience, the same for all human beings, is that experience is dependent on reality as well as upon the human mind.

Two factors, not one, enter into the composition of human experience: reality and the human mind. It is a product of their interaction—reality acting on our senses and our minds responding reactively by its perceptual and conceptual activities. The common core of human experience is the product of that interaction.

John Locke espoused a view of the human mind that had been held by almost all his predecessors in antiquity and the Middle Ages. That view regarded the human mind as a tabula rasa, a blank but impressionable tablet. The opposite view, introduced by Immanuel Kant, attributed to the human mind an innate structure, prior to all experience—forms of intuition and categories of the understanding—that shaped experience so definitely that our mind-determined experience, in effect, became an obstacle to our knowing the reality of things in themselves.

Only if the other view is correct, the view that the mind has no innate perceptual forms and no innate conceptual categories, can it be true that our mind-dependent experience does not preclude us from having knowledge of reality—of things in themselves—through that experience. What William James, in *Pragmatism,* called our commonsense categories were not like Kant's transcendental categories.

They were not a priori categories (in the mind prior to all experience). They were a posteriori categories (empirically derived, the product of much common human experience).

I must repeat here what I said in the preceding chapter about the perceptual activities of our minds. When we correctly declare ourselves to be perceiving something, we are at the same time affirming that the perceived object exists in reality. We cannot perceive nonexistent things, though we can be deceived into thinking that we are perceiving when, under pathological conditions, we hallucinate. The thirsty traveler in the desert hallucinates the mirage of a nonexistent waterhole, which he is deceived into thinking he perceives.

This being true, the question we must now confront is whether the perceived object that we affirm to really exist has in reality the character that it is perceived as having in our experience of it. To answer that question with an unqualified and unexceptional affirmative would be a naive realism. Commonsense realism may not be as critical as it should be, but neither is it that naive.

Things are not always as they appear to be. Our general acknowledgment of this simple fact leads to much philosophical sophistication about the differences between appearance and reality, but that sophistication should try to avoid the extreme of regarding all appearances as illusory. Only some are, as when the glittering vein in a rock is mistaken for gold or when a diamond-shaped bit of brilliant glass is mistaken for the real gem. Otherwise, the chair, dog, or tree that we perceive not only really exists and not only has the appearance of a chair, dog, or tree, but, in fact, that is what those three perceived objects really are. What they are *per se* (in themselves) is what they are *quoad nos* (for us).

Our perceptual experience has brought us into contact with the reality of these perceived objects—things that really exist and are what they appear to be. The explanation of why and how this is so requires us now to consider the conceptual factors that enter into our perceptual experience of really existing things.

In the first place, it must be understood that all of our normal perceptions are conceptually enlightened. From this fact arises the most radical difference between human perception and the perceptions that constitute the experience of all other animals. Their perceptual experience is conceptually blind, as human experience also is under the pathological conditions that produce agnosia.

I have discussed such conceptual blindness earlier (in chapter 3, p.18); the case of the man who mistook his wife for a hat, the person who could not see the streetcar the sound of which he could hear, or the person who could not see or feel the rose that he recognized by smelling. In all these cases, perception through the avenue of one sense is conceptually blind, but not through another sense. The intellect is cooperating in the perceptual activity through one sense but not in the perceptual activity of another. The pathologically affected patient is conceptually blind when seeing but not when hearing, when touching but not when smelling.

Except for agnosia, the human mind's perceptions are almost always conceptually enlightened, almost never conceptually blind. This means that the intellect normally cooperates with the senses in our perceptual activities or processes. But such cooperation on the part of the intellect need not lead to any distortion of our perceptions in one direction or another.

In scientific observations that are said to be "theory controlled" by one or another of several diverse hypotheses or theories, there may be conceptual coloration in several diverse tints that distort the perceptual process in one direction or another. But this is not the case in our ordinary perceptual experience. That is why I have spoken of our ordinary perceptual experience as being conceptually enlightened.

The concepts that enter into our perceptual experience divide into two classes or kinds. We recognize this division when we speak of certain ideas as being concrete and others abstract. That, of course, is a misstatement, for all ideas (i.e., all concepts) are abstract in the sense that their reference is to universal objects of thought, not to the singular objects of perception. The division intended by that misstatement is one between concepts that are capable of being instantiated in perceptual experience and concepts that cannot be thus instantiated (i.e., for which no perceptible instances can be found).

For example, the concept of chair, dog, or tree is instantiable perceptually, and that is why it is miscalled "concrete." In contrast, the concept of liberty, justice, or equality is not instantiable perceptually, and that is why it is miscalled "abstract."

This does not mean, for example, that we have no experience of liberty, but only that liberty is not something we perceive through our senses—our vision, hearing, touch, taste, and so on. Our concept of liberty is empirically derived even if that derivation cannot be attributed to sense-perception.

Divided against all empirically derived concepts, both those of which perceptual instances can be found and those that cannot be perceptually instantiated, there is still another class of ideas. Like concepts, their reference is to universal objects of thought, but unlike concepts, they are constructed by the intellect from concepts rather than being abstracted, as concepts are, from experience, perceptual or otherwise. These are called "theoretical constructs" by contemporary philosophers of science. Earlier philosophers called them "fictions of the mind" or *entia rationis* (beings of reason).

These different ways of referring to them call our attention to the same point: namely, that the object of thought to which they refer may or may not exist in reality and can never be perceptually instantiated or otherwise experienced. To discover whether or not the object referred to by such theoretical constructs as *neutrino, black hole,* or *God* really exists involves an elaborate process of inference, in which some perceptual experience may be involved, but the question is never settled by perceptual experience alone.*

My reason for calling attention to these various distinctions—between empirical concepts that can be and cannot be instantiated in perceptual experience, and between both

---

*I have described the mode of argument involved in affirming the existence of objects signified by theoretical constructs in another book, *How to Think About God* (1980), chapter 10, pp. 94–102, especially p. 98. In his effort to correct the fallacy of reification, William of Ockham formulated a rule of inference that warranted reaching the conclusion that certain imperceptible objects exist in reality. The rule applies in the same way to theological constructs as it does to the constructs of natural science.

kinds of empirical concepts and theoretical constructs—is to point out that when empirical concepts enter our perceptual experience through the cooperation of our intellect with our sensitive powers, they result in what I have called the conceptual enlightenment of our perceptions. Intellectual coloration and, perhaps, distortion occurs only in scientific observations that are theory-controlled and in which theoretical constructs, not empirical concepts, are involved in the intellect's cooperation with our sensitive powers in perception.

Before we consider the division of our experience into ordinary and special, it is necessary to set aside the portion of our ordinary experience that is private. All of our subjective experience is private—directly accessible to each individual person and to no one else. The realm of private experience includes, as we have seen, all our bodily feelings, our pains and pleasures, our emotions, our desires, our dreams, our fantasies, and our objects of thought when we engage in solitary reflection or meditation.

Only the latter might become objects that we share with others if we turn from private soliloquy to conversation about them with others. The objects of thought in our experience, whether privately considered or discussed with others, may also involve thought about things that really exist and are capable of being perceived or they may have their being only in the minds of those considering them. They may be *entia rationis*—beings or fictions of the mind.

Our private experience has little to do with the reality of the external world in which we live. It may give us some knowledge of our own bodies and of our personal selves, but most of its content is without any cognitive significance. Our cognitively significant experience is for the most part public—experience that we share with others and that is either common or special.

Our ordinary experience is the experience we daily have in the course of our waking lives and that, for the most part, we share with others, and so it is public rather than private. It is mainly our perceptual experience of the really existing things with which we interact as we go about our business and carry on our affairs. In addition to perceptual objects, it may include objects of memory, imagination, and reflective thought. For the most part it serves one or another practical purpose rather than the pursuit of truth or the attainment of knowledge.

This leads us to a negative point in the definition of our ordinary experience. It is experience we all have *without* its being directed by questions or problems like those that direct investigative efforts in scientific research or inquiry. It comes to us simply by our being awake and conscious and by having our senses acted upon. We make no effort to get it. We are not seeking to answer questions by means of it. We employ no methods to refine it. We use no instruments of observation to obtain it. In short, it is the experience that ordinary persons have and, for the most part, share.

The observations made by scientists in the laboratory or in the field obtain special data not to be found in our ordinary experience. The observational processes of scientific investigation are directed by questions to be answered, problems to be solved, hypotheses to be tested. The results obtained by those purposeful, methodical procedures, entailing elaborate apparatus, instrumentation, and other technical devices, constitute the special experience upon which the scientist depends in his efforts to obtain knowledge about reality, to separate false conclusions from true ones, and to ascertain the probability of his true conclusions.*

Not everything that belongs to the ordinary experiences of a particular person is shared by all other human beings. The ordinary day-to-day experiences of the twentieth-century

---

*See my prior discussion of ordinary and special experience in *The Conditions of Philosophy* (1968), chapter 7; and in *Ten Philosophical Mistakes* (1985), chapter 4, pp. 102–105.

Eskimo, New Yorker, and Hottentot are certainly not the same in all respects. The same may be said of an Athenian living in the fourth century B.C., a Parisian of the thirteenth century, and a New Yorker of the twentieth century. But their experiences do not differ in all respects. There are a certain number of things about which they could immediately communicate with one another if they were to meet and engage in conversation: such as the shift from day to night, some change in the seasons, living and dying, eating and sleeping, losing and finding, getting and giving, standing still and moving about, and so on.

I am assuming here that these communicators are persons of no special learning—persons whose minds have been untouched by science or philosophy. The aid of an interpreter may be needed for translation from one language to another, but that is all.

Those universally shared aspects of daily human experience that do not result from any special efforts to investigate or observe should be regarded as the core of common experience that unites all human beings on earth as participants in one and the same experienced world. This shared common experience includes not only perceived objects but also remembered past events and objects of thought that may or may not be instantiated in reality.

As the special experience that results from scientific investigations, observations, and measurements gives rise to scientific knowledge of reality when reflectively analyzed and interpreted by hypotheses and theories, so the common core of ordinary experience gives rise to our commonsense knowledge of reality, which may be elaborated on and refined by philosophical analysis and reflection.

When I said at the beginning of this chapter that although human experience is mind-dependent as reality is not, it is nevertheless the same for all human beings to a considerable extent, I had in mind what I have called the common core of ordinary experience that is public, not private.

Commonsense and philosophical realism, implicit in the statement that our common sense and philosophical knowledge of reality derives from the common core of our ordinary public experience, does not overlook the fact that that experience and that knowledge of reality is distinctively human. It is not the experience enjoyed and the knowledge attained by nonhuman animals, who have minds but not intellects and whose sensitive apparatus varies greatly from our own in many respects. Their perceptual experience of reality differs in its sensitive range and acuity from ours. None of it is enlightened by conceptual thought.

Perceptual objects, however, the existence of which we affirm when we perceive them, also really exist for other animals even though the way those objects appear to them may differ greatly from the way they appear to us. That raises a question. Does the way really existing things appear to us more nearly approximate their structure and character than the way these same things appear to other animals? I tend to answer this question affirmatively.

My reason for doing so is that our perceptual experience of reality is intellectually enlightened by commonsense categories and empirical concepts that are derived from the common core of our ordinary experience of reality; theirs is not. In addition, other animals are less likely to be able to correct all the tricks the senses play that result in deceptions rather than perceptions.

Human beings have learned how the senses produce illusions and hallucinations. They know how to correct or avoid them. They are, therefore, seldom misled into mistaking an illusory appearance for a veridical perception of reality, and if some persons are misled, others can always be found to correct them.

The experienced reality of the world in which we live is

not a construction of our minds, even though our experience of it is mind-dependent as its reality is not. In the course of human history many different worldviews—models or *versions of the world*—have been developed, varying from culture to culture, from time to time, and from one stage of scientific or philosophical speculation to another. In the contemporary world, this variety of worldviews or weltanschauungs also exists.

These are all products of the intellectual imagination. The plurality of worlds thus pictured or imagined should never be confused with the world that we perceive. Nor should these worldviews or world-pictures be assessed for their truth or falsity by their correspondence or noncorrespondence with reality and by pragmatic, empirical tests of such correspondence or noncorrespondence. If some are better and others worse, the only measure of that is the degree to which they can be harmonized and made coherent with our commonsense knowledge of reality, which, being based on the common core of ordinary human experience, is the same for all of us.

The kind of world-making or world-construction that I referred to in the preceding chapter when discussing recent books by Professors Goodman, Bruner, and others is not a cognitive activity at all. Its aim is not knowledge of reality. It may originate in experience, but it goes far beyond that in flights of fancy that are works of the intellectual imagination.

The world-pictures or world-versions thus produced are like the worlds produced in great novels and dramas that we regard as works of imaginative literature, not works of science and philosophy. Professor Bruner is mistaken in his notion that human cognitive activities can be divided into two modes: the explanatory or scientific, and the imaginative or narrative. The latter is not cognitive at all.

The ancients wisely distinguished poetic truth from scientific or philosophical truth. The measure of the latter was its correspondence with the actualities of the real world in which we live. The poetic truth of a story or narration lies rather in its internal coherence and in its conformity with the possible, not the actual. In short, if it is a likely story, believable because it might have happened, it has poetic truth.

Of the many different worldviews or world-versions that the human mind has been able to construct, some have more poetic truth than others, but none should be mistaken for or converted into the really existent world in which we live and that we experience from day to day. Nor should the construction of these fictions of the mind be confused with our efforts to attain knowledge of reality, either through ordinary common experience and the philosophical refinement of it, or through the special experience derived from scientific investigation and the development of scientific theories emerging about it.

CHAPTER 10

About How One Realm
of Meanings Underlies
the Diversity of Languages

IN CHAPTERS 8 AND 9, I defended the thesis of empirical realism: that the independent reality of the world in which we live is evident from our common experience of it. It is one and the same reality for all of us, and in the experience that we have of it there is a common core that we all share. This runs counter to the myriad forms of idealism that abound in modern and contemporary philosophy, which deny a knowable reality independent of the mind and which regard the mind's own structure or inherent forms and categories as constitutive of human experience. The plurality of worldviews that the mind constructs become a plurality of man-made worlds.

The problems we face in chapters 10 and 11 deal with the other side of the same coin. There may be one and the same reality for all of us and human experience may have a common core, but is the mind, and especially the intellect, of all human beings essentially the same? Is there one human mind, having specific properties common to all members of the human species, just as there are common anatomical and physiological properties common to all of us? Or is there a diversity of minds varying according to the diversity of languages in use and varying with the diversity of cultures in which the mind is reared?

In short, do human beings, living in the same real world, have divergent mentalities because of the diverse languages they use and because of the differing cultural conditions under which they have been reared? In the twentieth century that question is answered affirmatively by philosophers of language and by cultural anthropologists, and that affirmation lends support to the twentieth-century forms of idealism that we have considered in the preceding chapters. Against these mistaken views, I am going to try to defend the thesis that there is one and the same human mind in all members of the species, not a primitive and a civilized mind, not a Western and an oriental mind, not an ancient and a modern mind.

That thesis can be stated more generally by saying that no qualifying adjective preceding the word "mind" signifies an essential difference in the mind's powers and operations. The many different languages that human beings use result in superficial differences in the way they think, none of which is an insuperable barrier to communication. The many diverse cultures in which human beings are reared result in superficial differences in the habits they form and the customs practiced, none of which abolishes the common humanity that is most significantly represented by the human mind they all possess. In support of these contentions, I will deal with the diversity of languages in this chapter and the diversity of cultures in the next.

I have repeatedly used the word "mind" in the preceding

paragraphs, but it is man's intellect, not the human mind as a whole, with which I am mainly concerned. No one doubts that human beings everywhere and at all times have exactly the same bodily organs that constitute man's sensitive apparatus—the same brain and central nervous system and the same organs: visual, auditory, olfactory, tactile, taste, kinesthetic, and other sensory receptors. These are all anatomical properties, common to all normal members of the human species. Hence the sensitive powers of the human mind, including sensitive memory and imagination, are much the same in all human beings. The diversity of languages is unlikely to affect their operation to whatever extent their operation is not intellectually influenced.

However, to the extent that the way persons think and understand affects the way they perceive and imagine, basic intellectual differences among human beings will result in basic differences in their perceptions and imaginations. What I am contending, therefore, is that the diversity of languages does not produce basic intellectual differences.

In what respects are human languages diverse? First of all, they differ in the physical notations they employ in oral and written speech—the audible sounds and the visible marks they employ. Second, they differ in their grammar and syntax—the ways in which these sounds and marks are ordered to make sentences or statements. Third, they differ in the scope or range of their vocabularies—in the number of words and idiomatic phrases available for the communication of thought and to express experiences that may be either private or public.

Some languages may lack words or phrases that other languages possess for the expression of certain experiences or the communication of certain thoughts. The expression of experience and the communication of thought that is facilitated by the grammar and syntax of one language may be impeded by the grammar and syntax of another.

In all these respects languages differ, but underlying all these differences is something common to all of them: the meanings they convey when one human being engages in conversation with another. Without these meanings, the audible sounds uttered are just noise; the visible marks written, printed, or engraved are just nonsense doodling. Where do the meanings come from? Not from the audible sounds or visible marks, for they are transformed from meaningless physical notations into meaningful words by their acquisition of meaning. A meaningful word cannot acquire the meaning that its physical notation has come to possess from the meanings possessed by other words in the lexicon of a given language; for all the meaningful words in the lexicon language are so interconnected that no one word or set of words is capable of conferring meaning upon another word or set of words.*

What, then, is the ultimate source of all the meanings that are attached to the words that alphabetical languages use and to all the ideographs used in nonalphabetical languages? The only tenable answer is the human mind and especially the intellect.

Words acquire meaning, lose meaning, change meaning, and are for the most part ambiguous and have a variety of meanings. For these things to occur meanings must exist in and of themselves. Where? In the human mind and especially in its intellectual part.

There are two kinds of signs: signals, and referential signs. Referential signs are not signals in the way that clouds signal rain or smoke signals fire, but signs in the way that the word "cloud" signifies a visible object in the sky and the word "smoke" signifies a visible object on earth.

All words are one kind of referential sign, the kind that

*For a fuller analysis of the process by which meaningless physical notations become meaningful words and how this affects their lexical meaning, see an earlier book of mine, *Some Questions About Language* (1976), especially chapters 2–3.

is instrumental in the conveyance of meaning. Instrumental signs have two properties: one is the fact that they are themselves perceptible physical marks or sounds; the other is that to become words, those perceptible physical marks or sounds must acquire meaning.

If I may misuse the word "idea" to stand for the cognitive elements in the human mind—its perceptions, memories, images, empirical concepts, and theoretical constructs—I can then say that ideas are the other kind of referential sign. They are formal, not instrumental, signs. They differ from instrumental signs in two respects.

One is that they are themselves inapprehensible. As I have pointed out in an earlier chapter of this book, we are never, and cannot be, consciously aware of our own ideas, but only of the objects they refer to—not of our perceptions but of the perceptible objects we perceive; not of our memories but of the memorable events we remember; not of our concepts but of the intelligible objects we understand by means of them. In all these differing dimensions, the idea is not *that which* we apprehend, but *that by which* we apprehend its characteristic object.

The other respect in which ideas as formal signs differ from words as instrumental signs is that, unlike words that *acquire* and *change* meaning and can have many meanings, each idea *is* a meaning. Formal signs do not acquire meanings, change meaning, or have many meanings. Each is a single meaning, which is its reference to the object perceived, imagined, remembered, or understood. Words as instrumental signs get their meaning by being imposed upon the objects referred to by ideas as formal signs. By being thus associated with ideas, words *express* the meanings that ideas *are*.

Let me make this last point a little more explicit. The radical difference between words and ideas is the difference between *having* a meaning or *many* meanings and *being* a meaning and just *one* meaning. If the world did not contain entities that simply *are* meanings, each one just one meaning, then the world could not contain entities that *have* meaning, meanings they acquire, lose, and change.*

An idea cannot change its meaning or lose its meaning without ceasing to be the meaning that it is. An idea cannot be ambiguous, for to be ambiguous it would have to be several diverse meanings, which is impossible because that is tantamount to saying that one idea can become two or more ideas.

The human mind, and especially its intellect, is the realm in which meanings exist, the meanings that words acquire when they are imposed on the objects referred to by ideas. It can, therefore, hardly be the case that the different languages human beings use cause them to have fundamentally different minds and intellects.

The fact that a particular language does not contain words to express certain experiences or ideas or the fact that its syntax makes the expression of certain thoughts extremely difficult indicates defects that can be remedied.† It does not indicate that persons using that particular language have minds or intellects different in their fundamental powers from the minds or intellects of those using a language that has the requisite words and syntax.

Persons who have been reared using a defective language suffer from a nurtural not a natural defect. Nurtural

---

*Jacques Derrida's doctrine of deconstruction, as applied to the interpretation of the words on a page, is as self-refuting as the skeptical assertion that it is true (or that it is false) that no statement is either true or false. Because of that fact, I have paid no attention to the doctrine of deconstruction, but I would like to call attention to the fact that the account in this chapter of the relation of language to mind as the realm in which meanings exist goes a long way toward explaining the profound mistake made by the deconstructionists.

†Among the thousands upon thousands of human languages, any particular language may be defective in the respects indicated as compared with another particular language. I am not saying that some languages are perfect and others are defective.

defects can be remedied. Translation is the remedy that is always available. This may require the addition of words and phrases to a language that lacks them. It may require circumlocution that is cumbersome. It may require syntactical refinements and subtleties. But all these things are possible because any human mind can acquire the ideas possessed by another human mind.

Using ideas, any human mind can relate them to one another and order them in the same way that any other human mind can, and so there is a universal grammar that is inherent in the nature of the human mind and that underlies the plurality of conventional grammars that control the diverse modes of syntax in the plurality of conventional languages.

The simplest way of making the point that there are many human languages but only one human mind and intellect is to say that human beings can communicate with one another about anything. Communication may be difficult because of defects in the diverse languages that the persons may respectively use, but since those defects are always remediable, communication is always possible. It is always possible for one person to teach and for another person to learn the ideas that the one possesses and the other lacks.

If something is perceptible, any human being should be able to perceive it. If something is intelligible, any human being should be able to understand it. If something is thinkable, any human being should be able to think it. If something is knowable, any human being should be able to know it.

Of course, there are many exceptions to this statement of an ideal in principle. But they result from intellectual deficiencies or other mental impairments, such as sensory deprivations or loss of sensory acuity, never from language defects. Given adequate sensory equipment and adequate intellectual power, there are no unsurmountable obstacles to communication between one person and another, because what one of them can teach, the other can learn. Language defects may create difficulties in this process, but the difficulties are always remediable.

The ideal in principle thus remains: all conventional languages are completely translatable; all human experience (all that is public, not private) and all human thought are completely communicable. "To every fact which can be stated in one language, there will be a correlate which can be stated in another," Professor A. J. Ayer has written, going on to say, "There will be a loss of economy, but no loss of information."*

These two facts—universal translatability and universal communicability—attest to the universality of the human mind and intellect regardless of the diversity of human languages. Not only is reality one and the same for all human beings. Not only does our experience of that reality have a common core in which we all share. But by virtue of having the same human nature with the same species-specific properties, each of us has a mind and intellect that is essentially the same in all other human beings.

*"Philosophy and Language," in *Clarity Is Not Enough* (1963), p. 427. See also C. I. Lewis's *Mind and the World Order* (1920), pp. 94–95.

CHAPTER 11

About How the Plurality
of Cultures Springs from
the Unity of Mind

THERE IS another attack on the thesis that the human mind is the same in all human beings. This time the quarter from which the attack comes is mainly twentieth-century cultural anthropology. It is aided and abetted by twentieth-century existentialism in philosophy. A leading French existentialist, Maurice Merleau-Ponty, sums it up by saying that "it is the nature of man not to have a nature." It follows, of course, that if there is no specific nature, which all human beings share in common, then it cannot be asserted that they all have a human mind that is the same for all of them.

At first sight, two things are strange about this denial of human nature. First, what is alleged to be true of man is not ascribed to any other species of animal life. Each has a specific nature commonly possessed by all members of the species and having all the species-specific properties entering into the definition of the species. Why is the human species uniquely different from all other animal species by virtue of its not having a specific nature?

Second, neither the existentialists nor the cultural anthropologists can deny the well-known facts of anatomy and physiology. There can be no doubt that, anatomically, members of the human species have a large number of species-specific characteristics: one nose, two eyes, the same number of bones and teeth, the same structure of brain and central nervous system, the same number of chromosomes in their cells, the same genetic code, and so on. The same thing is true physiologically. These common anatomical and physiological properties are so clearly defined that no one could mistake a human corpse, freshly deceased, for that of any other species of animal.

These things being so, how shall we understand the denial that there is specific human nature? The answer lies in the facts to which the cultural anthropologists call attention: the extraordinary variety of behavioral patterns to be found in all the tribes and other societies that constitute human associations, and in all the ethnic, racial, and national groupings that differentiate one set of human beings from another.

Not only do all these subsets of the human population differ in their customs, their manners, their practices, their observances and rituals, their institutions, their tastes in food and dress, their sexual proclivities, their taboos or inhibitions, their family organizations, their arts and crafts, their forms of play and amusement, and their means of military aggression; but they also differ in their beliefs and prejudices, in their style of thinking and in the logic of their thinking, the manner in which they rear their young and educate them, their medical practices in the treatment of diseases, their religious dogmas, and their philosophical assumptions.

The existentialist philosophers go one step further. With regard to all behavioral matters, if not in anatomy and physiology, each human being is free to project and create his or her own individual nature. Individual human existence comes first, not the human essence or nature. Given existence initially, each individual forges his or her own nature on the anvil of his or her freedom.

That is what existentialists mean when they say that each human being is not born endowed with a specific nature, comprised of definite behavioral tendencies or propensities, instinctual drives or needs. All are free from birth to make of themselves what they can and what they will.

If the cultural anthropologists attribute a different cast of mind or a different mentality to each of the major and minor subsets of the human population, the existentialists appear to go even further. They endow each individual with the freedom to shape the character of his or her own mentality.

The response to these sweeping negations of one human mind that is the same in all human beings must begin by conceding that all the behavioral patterns that differentiate one subset of individuals from another, or even one individual from another, are of mental origin.

Since there are no instinctively determined patterns of human behavior, as there are in social insects and other lower animals; since all human behavior is learned behavior, which is not the case in other animals—it follows that the way human beings have learned to use their minds determines how they behave. Their different styles of behavior reflect acquired differences in mentality—in the ways their minds have been shaped by experience and by nurture.

It would appear to be the case that this initial concession gives away the whole case. Why, then, are the cultural anthropologists and the existentialists wrong in their denial of a specific human nature and a common human mind shared by all persons regardless of the subset of the human population to which they belong and regardless of their idiosyncratic individuality?

The answer is that they have failed to distinguish between potentiality and actuality, between innate powers and acquired habits, and between habitual dispositions to act in a certain way and the particular actions that individuals, having the same innate powers and the same acquired habits, diversely perform. These incredible failures in their understanding of human behavior, due to their ignorance of analytical insights so fundamental in ancient and medieval psychology, underlie their erroneous denial of a specific human nature and a common human mind.

What I have just said also accounts for their failure to understand the one point that they correctly make: namely, that the human species uniquely differs from all other species of animal life in not having the same kind of specific nature that all these other species have.

The specific natures of all other animal species are not only determinate in the anatomical and physiological properties common to all members of each species, but they are also determinate with respect to the actual patterns of behavior with which members of each species are innately endowed.

While the human species is like other animal species with respect to specific anatomical and physiological features, it differs from all others strikingly in the field of behavior. With respect to behavior, what is an actual innate endowment in the case of all other animal species is, in the case of the human species, only an innate endowment of potentialities.

All human beings have the same set of potentialities for behavior because the specific constitution of the human mind consists of the same set of passive and active powers—to be acted upon and to act in a variety of ways. All human beings have the same natural desires or needs, the same sensitive powers and powers of memory and imagination, and the same intellectual powers. These powers are the natural endowments that, along with common anatomical and physiological properties, constitute the specific nature of man.

The specific nature of the human species differs from the specific natures of other animal species by virtue of having behavioral potentialities or powers instead of behavioral actualities (i.e., actual patterns of behavior) among the set of attributes or innate properties that define the specific nature of the human species.

The innate nature of the human mind, consisting of these potentialities or powers, is the same wherever there are human beings—under all cultural conditions at all times and places. But that one and same human mind is nurtured differently under different cultural conditions. What the cultural anthropologists are describing when they report diverse patterns of human behavior in different subsets of the human population are all nurtural differences. These nurtural differences exist as acquired behavioral habits or dispositions. Underlying diverse habits are the same natural powers or potentialities.

Nurtural differences should never be interpreted either as natural differences or as a basis for denying the existence of a common nature. All the forms of racism and sexism with which we are acquainted have been prejudices bred by the error of attributing to nature what are only the products of nurture.

By correcting this error, Rousseau corrected one of Aristotle's most serious mistakes, the mistake of thinking that some men are by nature slaves. Those who are nurtured as slaves will appear to have slavish natures. Similarly, females nurtured as inferior human beings will appear to have natures inferior to males. It is this substitution of nurture for nature that causes the error made by cultural anthropologists and philosophical existentialists in the twentieth century.*

One more thing should be said on this subject. All the differences in the many, diverse conventional languages that manifest themselves in the ways that human beings express themselves are nurtural not natural differences. Such nurtural differences are superficial as compared with the underlying sameness of the human mind's natural powers. So, too, all culturally conditioned differences in human behavior are superficial nurtural differences as compared with the underlying sameness of specific human nature.

Here then is the correction of the mistakes made by cultural anthropologists in the twentieth century and by contemporary existentialists. To it must be added the correction, in the preceding chapters, of the mistakes made by contemporary philosophers of language and by the many forms of modern and contemporary idealisms.

There are still other matters concerning which ancient and medieval psychology give a much better account of the human mind than can be found in modern and contemporary psychology. That is mainly true with respect to man's intellectual mind, much less so with respect to the human senses, memory, and imagination. Hence we turn now to the consideration of the powers of the human intellect.

*For another discussion of this error, see Ten Philosophical Mistakes (1985), chapter 8.

PART III

The Powers of
the Intellect

CHAPTER 12

The Triad of Powers,

Habits, and Acts

IN ADDITION TO the anatomical and physiological traits that are the specific properties of the human body, human nature also has a set of innate potentialities for behavior. These potentialities are either active or passive: if active, they are powers to act in certain ways; if passive, they are receptive to being acted upon in certain ways.

In the history of psychology, the powers of the mind came to be called its "faculties." Treatises in which the analysis of the mind's powers occupied an important place were regarded as "faculty psychology."

The reaction against so-called faculty psychology occurred in the nineteenth century, initiated by Johann Herbart, a German psychologist and educator. From that point on, reference to the faculties of the mind gradually disappeared from the literature of psychology. Mention of them evinced a tendency to resurrect the outmoded psychology of Aristotle in antiquity and of his medieval disciple, Thomas Aquinas.

This much-touted revolution in psychology, regarded as a dismissal of erroneous ancient shibboleths by corrective modern insights and discoveries, arose from a basic misunderstanding of faculties. The word itself is a term originating with and used by psychologists since the seventeenth century. In the works of Aristotle and Aquinas, dealing with the behavior of living organisms, and especially with the actions of the human mind, the term used was not faculties but powers.

Neither natural powers nor the habits that are acquired modifications of them can be directly observed. In this respect, the powers and habits of the mind are like its cognitive elements, its ideas, when that word is used to cover the cognitive content of the mind—its percepts, memories, images, and concepts. To suppose that ideas are directly observable is the fundamental mistake of modern introspective psychology, from Descartes and Locke down to the end of the nineteenth century and until the first two decades of the present century, when behavioristic psychology first gained a foothold and subsequently replaced introspection.*

Just as mathematical physicists have come to deny the existence of those aspects of reality that they are not able to measure and thereby feed numbers into their equations, so introspective psychologists in the nineteenth century denied the existence of traits of the human mind that they could not observe introspectively.

At the same time, they mistakenly thought that they were looking directly into their own minds and finding all sorts of mental content there, which they then classified under a variety of headings. It is paradoxical, therefore, that they denied the existence of faculties because they could not introspectively observe them.

*See chapter 2 for a discussion of relevant considerations.

But what is not directly observable by one means or another may be inferrable, as the real existence of one's great-grandparents is inferrable from the direct awareness of one's own existence. It is from the acts or operations of the mind that we can infer both the mind's powers and also the habits that are acquired modifications of those powers.

Powers are potentialities. A habit is the first actualization of a power, determining the direction in which it is disposed to act. When the habit is operative in particular acts, we have an even more determinate actualization of the power to act.

Habits are formed by the repetition of particular acts. They are strengthened by an increase in the number of repeated acts. Habits are also weakened or broken, and contrary habits are formed, by the repetition of contrary acts. Acts of a certain type form or develop an acquired habit to act in a certain way. So different habits are different acquired perfections of a certain innate or natural power to act. In other words, there can be many acts of one habit, and many habits of one power.

Existentially, powers come first, habits second, and habitual actions last; and in origin powers precede acts, and acts precede habits, for it is by the operation of our powers that we form habits. In the behavior of mature human beings, most of the actions performed are habitual. It is very infrequently the case that intellectual action on our part issues directly from one of the intellect's powers that has not yet been habituated to act in a certain way.

The important point to note here is that habit stands in an intermediate position between power and act. From the variety of actions that we perform, we cannot directly infer the variety of powers that we possess, because different types of action may issue from different habitual dispositions of the same power rather than from different powers.

To infer the existence of different powers instead of inferring the existence of different habits will result in the mistake of multiplying the powers of the mind unduly. The number of different acquired habits is much larger than the number of innate or natural powers of the human mind. The unwarranted multiplication of mental powers, or natural faculties of the mind, may have been one cause of the attack upon faculty psychology.

The order in which we learn of the real existence of certain entities is the reverse of the order in which those entities really exist. Natural powers as principles of action precede in existence acquired habits as diverse perfections of those powers. Those acquired habits precede in existence the particular acts or operations in which they issue. But it is by first observing the actions of human beings that we can learn something about their natural powers and their acquired habits, being careful to proceed first from the observation of action to inferences concerning habits, and then proceeding by inference from acquired habits to natural power.

I said earlier that certain contents of the human mind— its perceptions, memories, images, and conceptions—are not directly observable by introspection. Other contents—such as bodily feelings, emotions, and desires—are elements in the private experience of each individual, and so are introspectively observable by that individual. Turning now from the contents of the human mind to its interior actions or operations, we find that those actions are directly observable as well as inferrable.

When the actions of the human mind issue in overt bodily behavior, that bodily conduct is observable in the same way that other phenomena are observed. From the observation of bodily behavior, which is the externalization of the mind's interior operations, we can infer the existence of those operations.

Much of that externalization may occur in speech behavior and then the validity of the inference depends on the truthfulness and accuracy of the speaker. Thus, for example, if a person truthfully and accurately reports to us what he has perceived through his senses, we can infer that a certain act of perception has occurred in his mind, and also that that act has produced in him a percept that neither he nor we can directly observe.

However, that person himself can directly observe privately what we cannot directly observe publicly. Each individual can be directly aware of the interior operations or actions of that individual's own mind. For example, I can be directly aware that I am engaged in the act of perceiving some object even though I cannot be directly aware of the percept by which I am perceiving it, but only of the object that I perceptually apprehend.

The percept that is produced by my act of perception is inapprehensible by me, as are all the other cognitive ideas in my mind. But I can be subjectively aware of the noncognitive elements in my private experience, such as bodily feelings, emotions, and desires. In addition, I can have direct awareness of all the actions of my own mind even though I cannot be directly aware of all the contents of my mind that those actions produce, specifically not of the ideas that are among the contents of my mind.

The point that I have just made is true of human beings, and not of other animals, because the human mind is intellectual and the intellect is reflexive. It knows its own existence reflexively and also its own operations, those operations that are purely intellectual as well as those in which it cooperates, such as sense-perception.

The intellect's reflexive knowledge of its own operations should not be confused with the misguided effort to know introspectively all of the mind's content, its cognitive as well as its noncognitive content.*

The way in which we can detect the presence of habits rather than powers is by appealing to one very simple criterion. If the type of observed action from which the inference is being made to either power or habit occurs in all human beings, then we are justified in inferring the existence of a power rather than a habit. What is common to all human beings must be a property of human nature, not a product of nurture or a result of action by some individuals but not by all. We know that habits are products of nurture. They result from *individual actions by some, but never by all.*

For example, some human beings think analytically but not all. The ability to think analytically is, therefore, an acquired habit not a natural power of the human mind. Faced with alternative options in the sphere of their overt behavior, all human beings choose freely, sometimes if not always. The ability to exercise free choice is, therefore, a natural power of the human mind, not an acquired habit.

I will attempt to apply this criterion for distinguishing between natural powers and acquired habits in the chapters that follow when I deal with the powers, habits, and acts of the human mind.

*The foregoing discussion elaborates further on the discussion in chapter 2 of the mind's unobservability. There the main point was that the cognitive contents of the mind—its percepts, memories, images, and conceptions—are *that by which* we directly apprehend perceived objects, remembered events, the fictions of the imagination, and the objects of conceptual thought, never *that which* we apprehend.

CHAPTER 13

Cognitive Power and Its Acts:

Conception, Judgment, Reasoning

ARISTOTLE'S *Metaphysics* begins with the words "Man by nature desires to know." Aristotle might have added that man's natural desire for knowledge as a good to be sought is realized by man's natural ability to learn and thereby to acquire knowledge.

In these two facts about human nature we have evidence of two basic powers of the human intellect: the appetitive and the cognitive. These two powers are irreducible. They are interactive and cooperative. Desiring is not knowing, but we cannot desire without knowing the object to be sought. Knowing is not desiring, but we do not learn very much without being impelled to do so by desire.

Being an animal with an intellect as well as senses, man shares with other animals additional powers—many sensitive powers and a locomotive power. The cognitive power in man is, therefore, twofold: sensitive and intellectual.

The appetitive power in man is similarly twofold. Man's desires are both sensual and intellectual. He has sensual desires that spring from or accompany his emotions or passions, as well as an intellectual appetite that is man's will.

The locomotive power that humans share with other animals underlies the sphere of all of man's overt behavior that expresses itself in the voluntary movements of the organs of his body. These are set in motion by his will and by his sensuous desires, two forms of appetite that sometimes cooperate but are more often in conflict. I will deal with their conflict and cooperation in chapter 15 on the relation of the passions to the reason; and in chapter 14, I will deal with man's intellectual appetite and with questions about his will and its freedom.

Before we turn to the intellect's cognitive power, it would seem reasonable to ask whether these two intellectual powers—the cognitive and the appetitive—exhaust the potentialities that having an intellect confers upon human beings. Subordinate divisions of each of these powers may have to be distinguished, and subordinate developments of each may occur through habit formation. But is there any third basic potentiality in human nature that, on the sensitive side, man shares with other animals, and, on the intellectual side, is uniquely his?

The answer is negative. In the history of psychology, modern as well as ancient, we find a threefold division of human consciousness and behavior into states or phases called cognitive, conative, and affective. The word "conative" covers the same ground for which I have used the word "appetitive." What does the word "affective" add? So far as emotions involve desires and drives that lead to action, the emotions are appetitive on the sensitive side of human consciousness and behavior.

What more is there that has been overlooked? The affects: feelings of pleasure and displeasure, satisfaction and dissatisfaction, contentment and discontent, elation and depression, and so on.

Do these affects point to a third natural power, either of the intellect or of the senses? I think not. In the preceding chapter I distinguished between active and passive potentialities and identified powers with active potentialities. The affects, in my judgment, are actualizations of a passive potentiality, not of a power, either intellectual or sensitive. They are all passions, minor or major.

The fact that the intellect's cognitive and appetitive powers cooperate in human action leads to the first distinction we must make with regard to the operations of the intellect in the sphere of its cognitive power. That is the traditional distinction between the speculative or theoretical intellect and the practical intellect.

The operations of the intellect's cognitive power—the power to apprehend, judge, and reason, to understand and know—are speculative or theoretical if the end for which they are performed is knowledge and understanding for their own sake. However, if they are performed for the sake of carrying out a decision or executing a choice in overt behavior that is activity in the pursuit of some goal, then the intellectual operations are practical. The distinction between the speculative and the practical intellect arises from the division of the intellect's cognitive operations into those two spheres according to the different ends they serve.

It was necessary to call attention to this distinction because the cognitive activities of the practical intellect are so different from the cognitive activities of the speculative intellect. Let us begin with a consideration of the latter.

Three quite different kinds of action exhaust the activities of the speculative intellect. All three are cognitive acts: they all eventuate in knowing or understanding. They are ordered serially, the first being indispensable to the second, and the second being indispensable to the third. These three distinct types of action indicate three specific divisions of man's generic cognitive power.

The first act of the speculative intellect is conception. Each act of conception is an intuitive apprehension of an object of thought. Calling it intuitive amounts to saying that it is nonassertive and nondiscursive. Calling it intuitive also makes this intellectual act analogous to the sensitive act of perception. As the former intuitively apprehends an intelligible object, so the latter intuitively apprehends a sensible object.

The second act of the intellect, employing the conceptions produced by its first act, is judgment. A judgment is assertive, not intuitive. It affirms or denies the relation between two objects of thought, expressed in the assertion that the intelligible object X does or does not stand in a certain relation to the intelligible object Y.

We need not be concerned here with the great variety of relations between intelligible objects that can be either affirmed or denied by our intellectual judgments, expressed in an equally great variety of propositions or statements. But we must note a basic distinction between two main types of intellectual judgments—judgments having or not having existential import.

In the sphere of sense-perception, I have pointed out on several earlier occasions that the act of perception is inseparably an act of apprehension and an act of judgment, at once both apprehensive and assertive. I cannot truthfully say that I apprehend something perceptually without at the same time making the judgment that that something really exists.

In this respect, intellectual apprehension and judgment differ radically from apprehension and judgment in the case of sense-perception. The two acts that are inseparable in the sensitive sphere are quite separate in the intellectual sphere.

When by conception I intuitively apprehend any intelligible object of thought, I always confront the question: Does that object exist in reality? I may not always be able to answer that question correctly, but I must always ask it because the mere apprehension of the intelligible object of my conceptual thought leaves quite open the question whether or not in reality there are one or more instances of it in existence. If I can answer that question affirmatively, I make an existential judgment that is true.

The first act of the intellect, whereby we apprehend an intelligible object of thought, is neither true nor false. It cannot be either because it asserts nothing. Only our intellectual judgments can be either true or false, for their assertion or denial that something exists, as well as their assertion or denial of a relation between this and that object of thought, can be tested for correspondence with what exists in reality and with the ways things are in fact related.

In the transition from conception to judgment, we pass from an intuitive and apprehensive act of the intellect to an assertive act into which conceptions enter as components, either asserted to exist or judged to be related in one way or another.

The next transition, from the second to the third act of the intellect, is from judgments to reasoning or ratiocination. It is a transition from a number of assertive acts of judgment to a discursive sequence of those acts in the process of inference.

All the many forms of valid reasoning and the many types of ratiocination involve inferences from one or more positive or negative judgments asserted to be true. These true premises cogently necessitate a conclusion—an affirmative or negative judgment—that must be asserted to be true.

Only acts of judgment are either true or false with certitude or probability. As we have seen, acts of conception, being merely the intuitive apprehension of intelligible objects (which may or may not exist in reality) are neither true nor false. We now see that the discursive process of reasoning or inference is also neither true nor false.

Reasoning or inference is valid or not, cogent or not, which means that, by the rules of one or another logic, it is correct or incorrect. When the reasoning or inference is correct, the truth of the asserted premises necessitates the truth of the conclusion. The truth of the necessitated conclusion is either certain or probable, depending on the truth-value attached to the premises asserted.

Not all judgments asserted as true are the conclusions of deductive reasoning, for if that were so there would be no assertible principles—no initial premises—and reasoning would be involved in an endless regress. Induction is the source from which reasoning takes its start. Induction itself is not a process of reasoning but rather an act of generalization from experience. In this respect it is like conception, which is an act of abstraction from experience.

The two kinds of induction that furnish the intellect with the principles or initial premises for deductive reasoning are intuitive induction and experimental induction. The few self-evident principles that we can assert as self-evidently true are the products of intuitive induction. From just one example of a triangle without diagonals in it and of a square with two diagonals in it, we can assert with certitude that no triangle can have diagonals in it. That is an intuitive induction of a self-evident truth.

Experimental induction is also intuitive in the sense that it is a generalization from a single instance—a carefully constructed experiment in which all relevant conditions have been controlled and from which all irrelevant factors have been excluded. Here the assertion of the generalization lacks the certitude of a self-evident truth because we can never be certain that the crucial experiment meets all the requirements of the ideal—*all* relevant conditions controlled, *all* irrelevant factors excluded.

There is a third kind of induction, which I shall call statistical, because unlike intuitive and experimental induction the generalization achieved is a judgment based on a large number of particular instances and upon an assessment of their frequency. If both positive and negative instances occur, the generalization will take the form of a statistical estimate of the probability that such and such is the case. An unqualified generalization that uses the word "all," as, for example, the judgment that all swans are white, can be falsified by one negative instance and replaced by a statistical estimate of the likelihood that more swans will be found that are white than are black.

When we say that some relatively few judgments are self-evidently true, we are saying that they are undeniable because it is impossible for the intellect to judge otherwise. Such self-evidently true judgments are also necessarily true and indemonstrable. Like the products of experimental induction, they are judgments that cannot be asserted as conclusions of valid reasoning or inference. Yet they can be regarded as knowledge.

Of the remaining judgments of the intellect, only those that are asserted to be certainly or probably true as the conclusions of valid inference or correct reasoning can be regarded as having the status of knowledge, either with certitude or probability. All judgments other than those that are self-evidently or experimentally true, or validly asserted to be true as correctly inferred conclusions, have the status of unsupported opinion, not that of certain or probable knowledge.

It is important for us to recognize this distinction between the judgments we make that have the status of knowledge and those that have the status of unsupported opinion. Some of our unsupported opinions may become supportable by effort on our part to discover the reasons for thinking them to have some measure of truth. That effort will succeed only if we can do the reasoning that turns what was before only an opinion into conclusions of a logically correct inference from premises that can be asserted as true judgments. For both the speculative and the practical use of the intellect, it is important to replace opinion with knowledge.

As I have already pointed out, we use such words as "thought" and "thinking" loosely when we talk about our intellectual activities. Greater precision can be introduced into our speech by identifying the act of thought with the first act of the intellect: the act of conception, or of apprehending intelligible objects. The process of thinking should be identified with the third act of the intellect: the discursive process of reasoning or inference.

The second act of the intellect—an existential or nonexistential judgment—should be identified with an act of knowing or opining. In distinction from acts of knowing or opining, what we call understanding should be identified with the first act of the intellect, for unlike knowing and opining, which always involve judging, understanding is always the intuitive apprehension of one or another intelligible object or object of thought.

We sometimes refer to intelligible objects as ideas, using that word for objects in our public experience, not in its subjective sense to refer to the private contents of our minds. I mention this to call attention to an important difference between knowing and understanding. Knowledge is always about matters of fact, never about ideas. Understanding is always of ideas. We do not *know* the ideas of liberty or of justice. We *understand* liberty or justice when engaged in the intellectual activity that consists in apprehending those intelligible objects conceptually. Judgments and inferences may follow such thought, but only for the sake of clarifying our conceptual understanding.

All the acts so far mentioned in the foregoing analysis of intellectual activity in its speculative dimension fall within the sphere of the intellect's cognitive power. Cognition is not confined to acts of knowing. It includes acts of thought and of thinking as well—acts of understanding and of reasoning or inference. Even the act of opining parades as a counterfeit of cognition.

When we turn from the speculative to the practical intellect, the same three acts—of conception, judgment, and reasoning—also occur, but with certain differences now to be noted.

The act of conception involves the understanding of intelligible goods. All the overt behavior to which activity on the part of the practical intellect leads is in the realm of good and evil, things to be desired or avoided, and, if desirable, things to be sought as ends or chosen as means.

The process of reasoning, often called deliberation in the practical dimension of the intellect, differs from reasoning or inference in the speculative dimension by virtue of its requiring two quite different kinds of judgment.

One kind is the same kind of descriptive judgment about matters of fact that, in the speculative dimension, we have classified as existential or nonexistential. The other kind, which is required only in practical reasoning, is a prescriptive judgment, a judgment that asserts what ought to be desired—what ends ought to be sought and what means ought to be chosen.

Descriptive judgments, either having or not having existential import, assert what is or is not the case as a matter of fact. In the sphere of the practical intellect, they assert what is in fact desired or not desired by human beings, individually or in groups. In sharp contrast, prescriptive judgments assert what ought to be desired whether in fact such things are or are not desired.

Not only are descriptive and prescriptive judgments clearly different, but so are the standards of truth that apply to them. The criterion of the truth of all descriptive judgments is, as I have said, the correspondence of the judgment with reality. There is no reality with which a prescriptive judgment can correspond. That is why some twentieth-century philosophers have concluded that all prescriptive judgments are mere opinions that cannot be tested for truth or falsity.

In the fourth century B.C., Aristotle proposed a standard of truth for prescriptive judgments. Instead of correspondence with reality, he proposed that a prescriptive judgment —an ought judgment—be regarded as true if it conforms to right desire. Right desire thus becomes the criterion for the truth of the prescriptive judgments that are involved in practical reasoning.*

The process of practical reasoning is more complex than the reasoning done in mathematics, in the theoretical sciences, and in speculative philosophy. Its greater complexity lies in the fact that it moves forward on three successive levels, whereas all speculative or theoretic reasoning occurs on the same level.

The highest of the three levels is the level of prescriptive principles: universal judgments about what ought to be desired or done. The second or intermediate level is the level of prescriptive rules about what ought to be desired or done. These are of general, but not universal, applicability. The third and lowest level is the level of prescriptive decisions about what ought to be desired and done in this or that particular case, here and now.

The reasoning involved takes the form of a practical syllogism that is formally the same on all three levels. In each case, the major premise must be a prescriptive judgment about what ought to be desired or done; the minor premise that accompanies it must be a descriptive judgment about a matter of fact that is relevant to what ought to be

---

*I have discussed this criterion and explained how it works in earlier books. See *Six Great Ideas* (1981), chapters 10–11, and *Ten Philosophical Mistakes* (1985), chapter 5.

desired or done. The conclusion reached by such reasoning is always a prescriptive judgment.

It is impossible to draw a prescriptive conclusion from two descriptive premises. From all the knowledge we might ever possess about matters of fact, we can never conclude anything concerning what ought to be desired or done.

Before I proceed to describe the sequence of all three levels of practical reasoning, let me give one example of a practical syllogism—one on the highest level. The major premise is a self-evident universal principle: the prescriptive judgment that we ought to desire everything that is really good for us and nothing else. The minor premise is the descriptive judgment about a fact of human nature: that human beings naturally desire knowledge, which makes knowledge something all human beings need and, therefore, something that is really good for them. From these two practical judgments, we can draw a prescriptive conclusion: the universal judgment that we (all human beings) ought to seek knowledge.

The truth of that practical judgment is in conformity with right desire because the major premise is a self-evidently true prescriptive judgment about right desire itself, and the minor premise is a true descriptive judgment about knowledge as something that all human beings naturally desire.

All practical syllogisms on the highest level of practical reasoning have universally true prescriptive principles for their major premise and for their conclusion. On the second or intermediate level, the major premise is a universal prescriptive principle that has already been established as a true conclusion of practical reasoning on the highest level. When that is combined with a descriptive judgment about contingent facts, the conclusion reached is a true general rule.

Then, on the third or lowest level, the true general rules that have been established as conclusions on the second level serve as major premises. Serving as minor premises are descriptive judgments about the facts of particular cases to which the rules apply. The conclusions that can then be drawn are sound practical decisions about what ought to be desired and done in this or that particular case.

The three levels of practical reasoning can be readily exemplified in judicial and jurisprudential thought. The highest level is that of the universal principles of natural law. On the next or intermediate level are the general rules of positive or man-made law in one particular country or another and at one time or another. The rules of positive law vary from place to place and time to time. On the lowest level is the application of those rules of positive law to particular cases that come before judicial tribunals for decision.

We can have certitude in our assertion of practical truth only on the highest level, the level of universal principles. On the intermediate and lowest level—the level of general rules and particular decisions—the soundness of the rules and decisions falls within the realm of doubt, less so about the correctness of the general rules than about the rightness of the particular decisions.

The importance of distinguishing between the three levels of practical reasoning and of prescriptive judgment is that it should help us avoid two mistakes that many persons make. One mistake consists in transferring one's doubts about the rightness of particular decisions, about which reasonable persons can disagree, to the universal principles that underlie those decisions and without which those decisions would be unprincipled.

The other mistake consists in regarding the universal principles on the highest level as irrelevant because of difficulties encountered in trying to apply them in making decisions in particular cases. There is no reason to abandon the universal principles of the practical intellect, about which agreement should be expected, because disagreement is unavoidable when reasonable persons argue about whether this or that particular decision is right.

Finally, I must deal briefly with one more distinction within the sphere of the practical intellect. That is the distinction between *praxis* and *poiesis*, which is a distinction between *doing* and *making*.

Thinking about the conduct of one's private life and about one's participation in the institutions and practices of the society in which one lives is thinking about *doing*, or thinking about one's moral and political actions. But to the extent that any of us exercises an art, technique, or craft to produce useful things or enjoyable objects, the practical thinking we are engaged in is thinking about *making*, not *doing*.

Here the universal principles of art, the general rules for producing a certain kind of work, and the particular decisions that the artist or craftsman must make in the process of production run parallel to the principles, rules, and decisions on the three levels of practical thinking in the sphere of *doing*—the sphere of moral and political action.

CHAPTER 14

Appetitive Power and Its Acts: Willing and Choosing

THE HUMAN INTELLECT has two generally distinct powers, as distinct as desiring is from knowing, as seeking is from understanding, and as judging and reasoning are from deciding and choosing.

The preceding chapter dealt with the intellect's cognitive power as distinct from the cognitive power of other animals, which resides in their sensitive organs; and as cooperative with the cognitive power of sense-perception, memory, and imagination. Here we shall deal with the intellect's appetitive power, which is traditionally called "the will."

The word "will" and many other words derived from it or associated with it are to be found in everyone's everyday speech. We speak of being willing or unwilling to do this or that. We confess to having a weak will or take pride in our strength of will. We talk about one person's willpower being greater than another's. We describe one action as voluntary and another as involuntary.

I suspect that few of the persons whose speech is peppered with these words realize that the will is an intellectual power or that the will is the intellect functioning appetitively rather than cognitively. Nor do they probably realize that the intellect in its appetitive dimension cooperates with sensual desires and emotional drives or urges, just as the intellect in its cognitive dimension cooperates with sense-perception, memory, and imagination.

The mentality of other animals also has two distinct powers: cognitive and appetitive. But lacking intellects, they do not have wills. Just as their cognitive powers do not rise above sense-perception and perceptual thought, so their appetitive powers do not rise above the level of sensual desire and the urges or drives of bodily passions or emotions. These sensitive powers, both in their cognitive and appetitive dimensions, are common to human beings and other animals.

Being animals, albeit intellectual animals, we, too, have sensual desires and emotional urges. These may come into conflict with reason and will, even overpowering them and causing us to act in a nonvoluntary fashion. Lacking intellects and, therefore, lacking wills, other animals always act in a nonvoluntary fashion, and by doing so, they do not exercise freedom of choice, as men do when they act voluntarily.

As the immateriality of the intellect in its cognitive dimension makes conceptual thought possible, so the immateriality of the intellect in its appetitive dimension makes the freedom of the will possible. If the will were embodied in a physical organ, such as the brain, physical causality would govern its actions.

The acts of the will are not uncaused acts, but the kind of causality that governs acts of the will, not being physical, permits them to be both caused and free. In the age-old controversy about free will versus determinism, it has seldom, if ever, been understood by those who take the determinist side of the issue that there is no conflict whatsoever between causal determinism in the realm of material things (bodies in motion), and free causation in the realm of the immaterial (acts of the will).

A central thesis of this book, as readers are fully aware, is that the brain is a necessary, but not a sufficient, condition of conceptual thought. We cannot think without our brains, but we do not think with them. This statement about the relation of the brain to the intellect's cognitive powers applies similarly to the relation of the brain to the intellect's appetitive power.

We cannot will our bodily movements without brain action, but freely willing to perform this or that bodily action is not an act of the brain. In the exercise of the intellect's appetitive power, as well as in the exercise of its cognitive power, the brain is only a necessary, but never a sufficient, condition.

In the nonvoluntary behavior of the higher animals, the brain and nervous system are not the only physical organs in which sensual desires and emotional urges are embodied. They are embodied in visceral organs as well.

Consider the difference between the behavior of a hungry cat meowing to be fed and that of a drowsy cat aroused by the sight of its food being placed on the floor. In the first instance, the cat's behavior is driven by hunger pangs in its viscera. In the second instance, the cat's behavior is driven by the visual perception of an object that arouses sensual desire on its part.

In the second instance, the desire that causes the cat to act is itself caused by a cognitive act—a sense-perception that involves the cat's eyes, central nervous system, and brain. In the case of the hungry cat, the hunger pang that arises in the cat's viscera innervates the cat's brain to meow for food.

Thirst and sexual urges operate in the same way as hunger. But while hunger, thirst, and sexual urges are present in both human beings and nonhuman animals, they do not operate in the same way.

In nonhuman animals, the behavior thus caused is always nonvoluntary. In human beings, with certain exceptions presently to be noted, the behavior that normally occurs as a result of such visceral urges is voluntary conduct in which the will is involved. For even when the impulse to act in a certain way is aroused by visceral urges, the action may or may not occur, depending on a free choice of the will to concur or not concur with the urge in question.

As we have seen, the nonvoluntary behavior of other animals is motivated in two ways: either by visceral urges of which the animal becomes sensitively aware, or by the sense-perception of desirable objects.

In sharp contrast, human voluntary behavior is motivated in only one way: always by a cognition of the object to be desired, whether that cognition is an act of perception and imagination in which the intellect cooperates or is purely an act of the intellect.

Seeing or imagining delectable food may cause a sensual desire for it that will be enacted if the will concurs in it. It will not be enacted if the will inhibits that sensual desire. But human voluntary conduct may occur without being precipitated by sense-perception or imagination.

Consider the human desires we call the love of pleasure or power, the love of money or fame, the love of liberty, of country, of God. All of these are intelligible, not sensible, objects. That is obviously true of power, fame, country, liberty, God; but it is also true of pleasure and money when these are not particular instances of pleasure or money, but pleasure and money in general.

I shall presently comment on the misuse of the word "love" to name these appetitive tendencies, most of which are acquisitive desires. The exceptions are patriotism, or love of country, love of one's friends, and love of God. In all these uses of the word "love," whether or not it is misused for acquisitive desire, the impulse to behave in a certain way is caused by an act of will, an appetitive act that is cognitively motivated. The object of desire is intellectually apprehended by an act of understanding, not sensitively apprehended by perception or imagination.

Though cognitively motivated by acts of intellectual apprehension, and also by acts of practical reasoning that may be involved in deliberation and decision about what action should be taken, the will's choice is not determined thereby. If emotion or passion does not overpower will and, in effect, put it out of operation so that the ensuing behavior is nonvoluntary, the will always remains free. No matter what prescriptive judgment issues from the practical intellect, the will always remains free to decide which course of conduct to command. No matter what choice is made by the will, if the behavior is voluntary, the will is always able to choose otherwise.

A person whom we love is a good example of an object of desire that, while it is an object apprehended by sense-perception, may be desired either sensually or intellectually. If the person is desired solely as a sexual object, then the desire is sensual, and both its arousal and satisfaction involve a variety of consciously felt bodily reactions and impulses. If the person is loved solely as a friend, then that love is purely an act of the will without any consciously felt bodily reaction; and that act of will takes the form of a benevolent impulse to confer all sorts of benefits upon the person loved.

One and the same person may be loved in both ways—as a sexually attractive person who arouses bodily impulses in us and as a friend toward whom our will is benevolently disposed. The love for that person is then erotic love, in which the sense and the intellect cooperate, quite different from mere sexual desire, which is lust and not love at all.

Love may be purely intellectual, having an object that is apprehended conceptually, and being the object of a benevolent impulse that is an appetitive act of will and not of sensual desire. Patriotism, the love of one's country, is one example; the love of God or of one's neighbor as one's self is another example of love that is intellectual in its appetitive aspect as well as in its cognitive aspect. It is an act of will that is not accompanied by any bodily feelings or reactions.

Acts of the will as acts of the intellect's appetitive power presuppose acts on the part of the intellect's cognitive power— acts of the practical intellect that are prescriptive judgments about what ought to be sought as ends and what ought to be chosen as means. After such judgments are made by the practical intellect, it still remains for the will to carry those judgments into execution by acts of intention with respect to ends and acts of choice with respect to means.

Since in the field of will's desirable objects, all objects desired are understood as either ends or means, the only acts of the will are the two just mentioned—intention and choice. Both are preceded by prescriptive judgments on the part of the practical intellect, but in neither case do the prescriptive judgments necessitate the act of the will in the way that, in cogent and valid reasoning, the premises necessitate the conclusion.

In this fact lies the freedom of the will: free in its intention of the end and free in its choice of means.

The will would be necessitated with respect to an intelligible object if the speculative intellect ever presented it with the apprehension of a complete and perfect good. That never happens on earth. Hence, both with respect to ends and means, the will is always free to intend and choose otherwise. Whatever the will elects as an end, it might have elected something else. Whatever the will chooses as a means, it might have chosen otherwise. In that one word—"other-wise"—lies the essence of the will's freedom.

As I have already pointed out, when strong visceral urges completely dominate our behavior and the will is temporarily in abeyance, our conduct is nonvoluntary. Such abnormal behavior on our part is exactly like the normal behavior of other animals. When that occurs, persons usually say that they would not have behaved in that way if they had not temporarily lost their minds; by which they mean that they would not have acted in that way had bodily urges or passions not temporarily been in complete control of their conduct.*

Even when we act voluntarily and the will is engaged in such action, the will may be more or less free. These degrees of freedom vary with the degree to which, on the one hand, rational judgments on the part of the practical intellect solicit the will's choice or, on the other hand, the degree to which sensual desires and bodily urges do.

In either case, the will remains free in its choice and the ensuing action remains voluntary. But when rational judgment prevails, the will's natural freedom of choice is augmented by its freedom from the passions. When the solicitation of sensual desires or emotions prevails, the will's natural freedom of choice is diminished by its subjection to the passions.

This loss of freedom is usually ascribed to what has traditionally been called a conflict between reason and the passions. The conflict might be more accurately described as between the prescriptive judgments of the practical intellect and the appetitive impulses of strong sensual desires or violent bodily emotions. The factors in conflict contend with one another in exerting influence upon acts of the will. If the

*Drug or alcohol addiction also produces in human beings such abnormal behavior. All addictive behavior is nonvoluntary.

influence of sensual desires or bodily emotions becomes dominant in this conflict, the will remains free, but reason does not control our behavior. If the prescriptive judgments of the practical intellect become dominant, the will remains free and reason controls our behavior.*

Sensual desires and bodily emotions are not always in conflict with rules of reason—prescriptive judgments of the practical intellect. They sometimes reinforce those judgments and generate impulses that tend in the same direction as the will's free acts.

Within the sphere of the intellect's appetitive power, habits are formed by repeated voluntary acts in one direction or another. When such habits result from voluntary acts in which reason controls the passions (i.e., the prescriptions of the practical intellect dominate), the habits are called "virtues." When, on the other hand, such habits are formed by voluntary acts in which the behavior has been dominated by uncontrolled sensual impulses, the habits are called "vices."

Sensual desires for food, drink, and other bodily pleasures aim at objects that are really good. Human beings need them, but not in unlimited quantities. Such desires become inordinate and lead to immoderate sensual indulgence when reason puts no limit upon them; and habits of immoderate sensual indulgence become the vices of gluttony, insobriety, and lust.

Of the three cardinal moral virtues, only justice is purely a habit of the will. The other two—courage or fortitude with respect to pains of all sorts and temperance with respect

*The titles of the last two books of Spinoza's *Ethics* illustrate the point just made. The title of Book IV is "Of the Passions, or of Human Bondage." The title of Book V is "Of the Reason, or of Human Freedom." What is called "moral liberty" by other philosophers and by theologians in the Western tradition consists in our ability to will as we ought in accordance with the moral law and the prescriptions of reason. Described negatively, moral liberty is freedom from the influence of the passions—sensual desires and bodily emotions.

to pleasures of all sorts—are habits of the passions or sensual desires as well as of the will. They are habits of the will insofar as the will acts freely in accord with the prescriptions of the practical intellect. They are at the same time habits of the passions or sensual desires insofar as their impulses have been moderated by reason, and they are thus prevented from being habits of inordinate sensual indulgence.

I have repeatedly referred to bodily emotions and sensual desires. I have used the word "bodily" to signify that, properly understood, emotion is a passion that the body suffers and we consciously experience when a complex set of bodily reactions occurs: changes in respiration and pulse, changes in epidermal electricity, increases of blood sugar and adrenaline in the blood due to reaction on the part of the glands of internal secretion, pupillary dilation or contraction. In short, an emotion is a widespread, violent bodily commotion that is consciously experienced and accompanied by strong impulses to act in a certain way.

When emotion is thus defined and understood, there would appear to be only two violent bodily emotions that we experience: anger and fear.* The sexual passion that occurs when sexual desires are consummated may be a third, but it is seldom as violent or as widespread a bodily commotion as anger or fear.

Readers may ask, "What, then, about all the words in everyday speech that appear to be the names for a much larger number of emotions or affective states than the two or three just mentioned?"

Literature as well as everyday speech is full of such terms as joy, sorrow, grief, compassion, sympathy, delight, depression, elation, and so on. Most of these terms signify affects that are states of the will, of which we are consciously

---

*Rage may be a better name for the violent emotion of anger, and "righteous indignation" a better name for anger when it is an act of the will without bodily involvement.

aware, but there is little or no felt bodily commotion in our consciousness of them.

Grief and depression are, perhaps, exceptions to what I have just said. A grief-stricken person is often convulsed with tears, sobs, and sighs or cries. A depressed person experiences loss of muscle tone, postural changes, and altered facial features. But for the most part, the list of words that are thought to be the names of emotions, sentiments, or affects (it could be much longer than the enumeration above) name literary inventions or fictions of the imagination. They are not names for experienced bodily feelings. They may be states or tendencies of the will that we experience consciously, but they are not accompanied by bodily feelings of any sort.

Most of us frequently misuse the word "hate," as if it were a strong bodily emotion, when we should instead use the word "dislike" to signify a state or tendency of the will. We use the word "hate" when we dislike someone intensely enough to wish to avoid any contact with that person. Such intense dislike, being an act of the will, is not accompanied by any bodily feelings. However, if the intensity of the dislike erupts into violent anger or rage, then a bodily emotion is felt and impulses to bodily action occur that may cause injury or death to the person emotionally hated.

The word "love" is similarly misused, often when no felt bodily emotion or sensual desire is experienced. In such cases, it would be better to use the word "like" when the intellectual judgment is simply one of approval. And as I pointed out earlier, we often misuse the word "love" when our appetitive tendency, sensual or intellectual, is one of acquisitive desire, not benevolent impulse. That is lust, not love; and it may lead to the violent bodily commotion known as orgasm.

In the chapters to follow, we will be concerned with the misuse and neglect of the intellect, as well as with the kind of habits that put the intellect to good use. Habits of using the intellect properly are the intellectual virtues. The contrary habits, formed by repeated misuse of it, are the intellectual vices. A very special vice, to which I have given the name "sloth," results from the nonuse of the intellect—from the habitual neglect of it.

The discussion in this chapter of the moral virtues, especially courage and temperance, prepares us for the consideration of the intellectual virtues. Without the fortitude needed for taking pains and surmounting difficulties, and without the temperance needed for restraining sensual indulgence and moderating the desire for sensual pleasure, it is unlikely that one would have the strength of character required to acquire the intellectual virtues.

PART IV

The Use, Misuse, and Nonuse of the Intellect

CHAPTER 15

Intellectual Virtue and Vice:
The Order and Disorder
of the Passions

I TRUST readers remember an important difference between the intellect's powers and its habits. Its powers are to be found in all human beings regardless of the circumstances of time and place and regardless of the use they make of these powers. The difference between habits and powers is that some human beings have habits others do not possess, resulting from the fact that some repeatedly perform actions that others do not perform at all or perform infrequently. Since every virtue is a habit formed by repeated acts, some human beings have virtues not to be found in others.

In the preceding chapter, while discussing the conflict between the passions or emotions and the will, I had occasion to refer to moral virtue as a good habit of both the passions and the will, good because it resulted from behavior in which rational deliberation and decision controlled our voluntary conduct. It is also good because, the habit being thus formed, it disposes us to act habitually in that way. The habitual disposition to act under the dominant influence of the passions is moral vice.

In that context I mentioned courage, temperance, and justice as if they were three distinct moral virtues, existentially separate so that it is possible to have one of these virtues without having another. I must now correct that impression. Courage, temperance, and justice are three aspects of moral virtue, analytically distinguishable from one another but not existentially separable. We are either morally virtuous or not; but if we are, to whatever degree, we have those three aspects of moral virtue to that degree.*

The reason why I call attention to this point is that in this respect intellectual virtue differs from moral virtue. There are a number of distinct intellectual virtues that I shall enumerate presently. One can have one or more good intellectual habits without having all of them.

There is another respect in which moral and intellectual virtues differ. For every aspect of moral virtue, such as temperance, the person who lacks that aspect has in its place an aspect of moral vice. For example, the person who is *not* habitually temperate *is* habitually intemperate.

In addition, such intemperance takes one or another of two opposite forms. One is an excessive habitual indulgence in the pleasures of the flesh. The other is the opposite extreme of defect: abstinence or abstemiousness with regard to such pleasures. The virtuous habit with regard to sensual pleasures stands in the middle between the two extremes of excess and defect. It disposes the person having that habit to

---

*I have explained elsewhere the reason why there is not a plurality of existentially separate moral virtues, but only moral virtue with analytically distinct aspects that cannot exist in separation from one another. See *Reforming Education* (1989), pp. 259–60.

behave moderately, indulging in sensual pleasure neither too much nor too little.

In all of the foregoing respects, intellectual differs from moral virtue. There is a plurality of intellectual virtues—good habits in the use of the intellect. Intellectual virtue does not stand in the middle between the extreme of excess and the extreme of defect.

Before we attempt an enumeration of the various intellectual virtues, let us consider the variety of ways in which we can put our intellects to good use.

One good use that should be mentioned at the outset is the use of the intellect's reflexivity to know and understand our own intellectual nature, which involves understanding the minds of others as well.

Another good use of the intellect is to understand our sensitive powers and to know their limits and defects.

A third is using the intellect for purposes that the senses do not serve: distinguishing between knowledge and opinion, judging the claims that are made with respect to the truth and falsity of assertions, and assessing the certitude or degree of probability that can be attached to assertions accepted as true.

Much of the knowledge that we attain is knowledge of reality—of the external physical world, of the social as well as the physical environment, and also of ourselves and other human beings. But these actual existences do not exhaust reality. Reality includes not only what actually exists now and what has actually existed in the past, but also what may or may not exist in the future as well as what may never come into actual existence at all. It includes the realm of the possible as well as the realm of the actual. The intellect should be used to explore the realm of the possible—to know what possibilities there are and to understand them.

It almost goes without saying that the intellect should be used to communicate effectively, to engage in intelligent conversation about basic ideas and issues, and to solve problems, both theoretical and practical problems. Most of these things cannot be done at all by the use of our sensitive powers, or, if done at all, not without the cooperation of the intellect.

We should make good use of the intellect in its practical dimension by deliberating well about ends to be sought and means to be chosen, by making sound judgments about such matters, and reaching pragmatically good decisions about them, both in the sphere of *doing* (the private and public conduct of our lives) and in the sphere of *making* (the production of useful or beautiful things). In the latter respect, we should cultivate our intellectual imagination, for that is indispensable to all productive, or, as it is sometimes miscalled, creative activity.

In the theoretical or speculative dimensions of the intellect, we should make good use of it by reasoning cogently and validly, by being able to argue well in defense of our fundamental convictions and beliefs, to engage in debate with others without being contentious or disputatious, to detect our own mistakes as well as to discern and criticize the mistakes of others. In doing this, it is most important to detect contradictions, whether apparent or real, and to discover on which side of the contradiction the truth lies, recognizing that it must lie on one side or the other.

Finally, in the pursuit of truth, we should use our intellects to attain some grasp of what is most fundamental—first principles, both in the theoretic and the practical order of our understanding.

The intellect, and the mind of which it is the best part, is our most treasured human possession. Making good use of it is, therefore, indispensable to leading a morally good human life. Thinking well is prerequisite to living well. If, as I think is the case, we are under a moral obligation to try to make good lives for ourselves, and to enrich them by making the most of our innate potentialities, then making the best possible use of our intellects is essential to that effort.

The preceding enumeration of the ways in which the intellect should be put to good use prepares us for naming the intellectual virtues. If we could exhaustively name them, that would cover all the good uses just mentioned.

Aristotle tried to do this in the fourth century B.C. He named five intellectual virtues, three good habits of the speculative intellect, and two good habits of the intellect in its practical dimension.

The Greek words he used to name the three speculative virtues were *nous, epistemé, sophia*. Translated into English, they are understanding, knowledge, and speculative wisdom.

The Greek words Aristotle used for the two virtues of the practical intellect were *techné* and *phronesis*. The English equivalents here are art or skill and prudence or practical wisdom.

Aristotle's enumeration calls for some comment. Understanding involves insight concerning intelligible objects—the most important objects of thought, or basic ideas using that word in its objective sense. Knowledge includes all branches of learning—historical, scientific, mathematical, and philosophical knowledge, the latter in addition to the philosophical clarification of our understanding of basic ideas. Speculative wisdom can be attained only by carrying our philosophical thought as far as possible—to the knowledge and understanding of first principles. This may require us to go from natural philosophy to metaphysics and to the conclusions it reaches in philosophical theology.

Art is the name for any skill or technique. It includes all the useful, liberal, and fine arts, or arts of the beautiful. When the word "art" is commonly used (I would say misused) for works of fine art, it obviously does not name an intellectual virtue—a habit that is possessed by human beings who are rightfully called artists, craftsmen, or skilled workers.

Prudence, or practical wisdom, is the name for sound thinking about particular means to be chosen here and now. It involves taking counsel, engaging in rational deliberation, and reaching pragmatically sound judgments about what decisions should be made.

Prudence, or practical wisdom, is a sound use of the intellect for the sake of morally good conduct. It is, therefore, the one intellectual virtue that is an inseparable aspect of moral virtue. One cannot be morally virtuous without being prudent also, and one cannot be prudent unless one is morally virtuous. The means one prudently chooses must be means to the right end appointed by moral virtue. If the ends for such means chosen are themselves immoral, the skill employed in choosing them well is not prudence, but cunning, cleverness, or craft.*

Thus understood, Aristotle's enumeration of the intellectual virtues would appear to be adequate. It is difficult to think of what more might be added. But the exhaustiveness of that enumeration is not what may be bothersome or troubling to twentieth-century readers. Aristotle himself could be a specialist in almost all the empirical sciences of his day as well as a generalist in his philosophical thought.

In our age of intense specialization in all fields of science as well as in history and philosophy, that is impossible today for anyone. It may still be possible for one to be a generalist in one's philosophical understanding of history and in one's philosophical understanding of basic ideas and issues.

No one today can be a specialist in all fields of history,

*I must qualify something I said earlier. I said that, unlike the aspects of moral virtue, to each of which is attached two vices that are the extremes of excess and defect, the intellectual virtues do not have pairs of vices attached to them. This is true of all the intellectual virtues except prudence, which, because it is inseparable from moral virtue, does have a pair of vices attached to it. At one extreme is habitual rashness—making decisions without the deliberation. At the other extreme is indecisiveness, which consists in being habitually unable to make decisions.

the whole range of mathematics, and in all the empirical sciences. No one can be a specialist in all the fine arts or all the useful arts. Only the liberal arts, which consist in a disciplined and skilled use of the intellect to read, write, speak, and listen well, should be in everyone's habitual possession.

A twentieth-century enumeration of the intellectual virtues, and one that is applicable to most human beings, not just the few who belong to an intellectual elite, is tantamount to saying what should be the good intellectual habits that a generally educated person should have acquired in the course of a lifetime of learning, especially in one's later and more mature years.

The attained intellectual virtues of the generally educated person in our society and in our century would include, first of all, a habitual possession of the liberal arts—the skills of thinking and learning so indispensable to knowing and understanding. Among the intellectual virtues would be a habitual understanding of the great ideas and issues, and a generalist's understanding of mathematics, the natural world, human history, and human society, acquired by a philosophical approach to the subjects named and accompanied by some knowledge in these fields of learning.

Included also would be an understanding of human history, human nature, and human society through a thorough acquaintance with poetry, especially narrative and dramatic fiction. If possible for some, if not for all, the generally educated person might also be a well-trained specialist, in one or two of the productive arts, as well as in some phases of history, in one or another empirical science, and in one or another branch of mathematics.

So far I have not mentioned the attainment of wisdom in the speculative dimension of the intellect and of sagacity in its practical dimension. In both dimensions, the opposite is folly, which, if persistent and habitual, must be regarded as an intellectual vice. What about ignorance and error, readers may ask; and also what about the defect that William James in a revealing essay called a "certain blindness in human beings"? All three of these are intellectual defects rather than vicious habits.

Of these three, ignorance, being a privation of knowledge, is more easily remedied than error that, if obdurately resistant to correction, proves to be an obstacle to learning.

The most serious of these defects is the intellectual blindness about which William James wrote. It is caused by strong intellectual prejudices that bar the reception of ideas contrary to the prejudices obstinately held. If irremediable, such blindness becomes an intellectual vice.

If a person suffers from the vice of folly and the vice of a closed mind, or intellectual blindness, the cause probably lies in what I regard as the most fundamental of all intellectual vices. That is the habitual tendency of a person to think emotionally—with his hips or his guts—instead of thinking rationally with his intellect.

Anyone who wishes to think rationally should have the habit of thinking coolly, with all affective feelings or sentiments and all emotions parked outside. The heat of the passions, especially if they are strong and violent bodily commotions, cannot help but cause a disturbance or even a distortion of all intellectual work.

William Wordsworth, in the preface to the 1800 edition of *Lyrical Ballads,* said that "poetry is emotion recollected in tranquility." No statement could be more significant about the role of the emotions in the work of the intellect. Emotion has its place in poetry, as well as in music and the visual arts, but that place is in the past, to be remembered, not in the present while the artist is engaged in the production of a poem, a musical composition, or a work of visual art.

What Wordsworth said about poetry applies not only to music, painting, and sculpture but also to mathematical and philosophical thought, to scientific research and reflection, and to historical inquiry. The less emotions cloud and bemuse the intellectual processes involved in all these pursuits, the better the results are likely to be.

I might add that the same thing is true of the intellect's involvement in political enterprises, especially with regard to international affairs, and also in bussiness and industry. What Barbara Tuchman called "the march of folly" throughout history can be attributed mainly to the intellectual blindness that emotional prejudices cause.

Emotional thinking is, to use Freud's phrase, "wishful thinking"—controlled by the drive of subjective desires and passions rather than by the objective realities to which dispassionate thinking should respond. Paradoxically, and obviously not recognized by him, Freud is caught in self-contradiction at this point.

If psychoanalytic theory claims that its hypotheses can be empirically verified or falsified by the data obtained by scientifically conducted, clinical research, then psychoanalytic theorizing is not wishful thinking. Yet Freudian psychology also claims that the passions control all human thinking, which is therefore wishful thinking throughout. Both claims cannot be true.

While thinking, to be done well, should be dispassionate in the sense of not being directed or controlled by emotions or other affects, it should also be passionate in the sense of enlisting emotional support for the conclusions reached.

One should have a passionate attachment to the conclusions of which one is convinced or persuaded, but emotions should not be involved in the ratiocinative process itself by which these conclusions have been reached. Nor should that passionate attachment cause one to be deaf to criticism and inhospitable to correction if the conclusions are not beyond the shadow of a doubt and so are open to challenge and question.

What I have just said about the conclusions of which we are convinced or persuaded is even more applicable to the assumptions, often hidden rather than acknowledged, with which we begin. It is here that an emotional investment in these assumptions is likely to prove an obstacle to an open examination of their truth or tenability. Nevertheless, from my long experience in teaching and lecturing, I know that the teacher or lecturer who does not express his convictions with passion or strong feeling is likely to be less effective than the one who does. It is in the expression of one's convictions, not in the thinking that produces them, that emotion can play a useful role.

Finally, I must return to a point made earlier when I said that moral virtue or strength of character is prerequisite to the acquirement of good intellectual habits. Here I must add that moral vice, or lack of a good moral character, is the cause of the intellectual defects and vices that we have considered.

CHAPTER 16

The Neglect
of the Intellect: Sloth

IN THE PRECEDING CHAPTER, I treated the use and misuse of the intellect. In this chapter, I propose to consider the disuse or nonuse of the intellect, for which the most appropriate name is sloth.

That English word is the translation of a Latin term in the Christian catalogue of mortal sins set forth by St. Gregory the Great. It also became the name for an almost completely dormant mammal that is usually found hanging by its claws on the branch of a tree. Because of this latter identification, sloth has in ordinary speech come to signify gross physical inactivity. In borrowing that term from both ordinary speech and from theological discourse, I have adopted it to designate an almost total neglect of the intellect or an inadequate use of it.

In the catalogue of mortal sins, sloth stands for spiritual lethargy or torpor. With their connotation of deep sleep, the words "lethargy" and "torpor" may be inappropriate for what I mean in using the word "sloth." But what I have in mind is conveyed by emphasis on the spiritual, not physical, dimension of our conduct. It is the intellectual, not physical, inactivity of a person for which I am using the word "sloth."

The ideal of intellectual virtue portrayed in the preceding chapter can be approximated in some degree by anyone who has the ability and willingness to make the effort. There are some human beings who, because of minimal or defective intellectual endowment, may not have the requisite ability. But there are a great many more who have sufficient ability to make the effort and fail to do so. It is those persons that I am charging with the fault of not using their intellects in the proper fashion.

Sloth is a moral fault, but unlike injustice that results in misconduct toward others, sloth is a moral fault that causes the misconduct of the individual's private life. In this respect, it is more like the lack of temperance, which is abstinence from sensual pleasures or the lack of fortitude, which is a habitual unwillingness to take the pains involved in doing what one ought to do for the sake of leading a morally good life.

One ought to make good use of one's intellect in order to lead a morally good life. Stated another way, one ought to lead an intellectual life. But many of us do not lead intellectual lives. Many of us are anti-intellectual. Many do not use their intellects beyond those uses they cannot avoid— its cooperation with the sensory powers in acts of perception, memory, and imagination.

If they go beyond such cooperative uses of the intellect, which confer conceptual illumination upon the things we perceive, remember, and imagine, they do not use their intellects for the purpose of increased knowledge and augmented understanding, sought for their own sake and not for some ulterior, practical purpose. They do not engage in the pursuit of truth for the love of it and for no other reason. They do not count the sheer delight of thinking well among the joys they prize and seek.

Those who do not lead intellectual lives deploy their intellectual powers in the work-a-day world of earning a living for the sake of getting ahead in that world. If they were not compelled to use their intellects for that purpose, they would not be inclined to do so. When they are not immersed in the economic rat race, they resort to various forms of play and entertainment for the sake of recreation from the fatigues of toil or in order to kill the time that lies heavy on their hands. It never or seldom occurs to them to use free time for the exacting pursuits of leisure instead of for recreation or the pleasures of play.*

The pleasures of play are intensified by great skill in one's participation in whatever sports or games to which one is inclined. One has to use one's intellect to acquire such skill. But that use of the intellect, taken together with its use for economic or even political advancement, is hardly a sufficient use. While it is not total abstinence from intellectual activity, it is certainly an inadequate employment of whatever degree of intellectual power we have.

In sharp contrast, what I have called the exacting pursuits of leisure are all forms of intellectual activity in which the intellect is (1) used productively in making things that are useful and enjoyable, (2) used practically in making judgments about things to be done for the sake of a morally good life, and (3) used speculatively in the pursuit of truth and in all forms of learning for the sake of gaining knowledge, understanding, and wisdom.

These three uses of the intellect will, if they become habitual, confer upon a person the intellectual virtues that

---

*I have in an earlier book discussed at length the difference between leisure-work and subsistence-work, one for the sake of personal improvement, the other solely for the sake of economic necessities. Both forms of work are quite distinct from all forms of play and amusement. See *A Vision of the Future* (1984), chapter 2.

Aristotle named in Greek antiquity—art and prudence, understanding, knowledge, and wisdom.

On the part of those who have sufficient intellectual ability to do so, sloth is either a habitual reluctance to employ one's intellectual power adequately, or it consists in almost total abstinence from an active engagement of the intellect in pursuits of leisure.

Anti-intellectualism gives rise to the most extreme, the most morally deplorable, form of sloth. It is to be found in persons for whom the ultimate objectives in life are the maximization of pleasure, money, fame, or power and who, thus motivated, express their contempt for those who waste their lives in purely intellectual pursuits. It is almost as if they wished they did not have the burden of having intellects that might distract them from their fanatical devotion to nonintellectual aims.

It is man's glory to be the only intellectual animal on earth. That imposes upon human beings the moral obligation to lead intellectual lives. The slothful are blind to the glory and neglectful of the obligation.

The Message of This Book

YEARS AGO, when, at the University of Chicago, Robert Hutchins and I led great books seminars for undergraduates, President Hutchins would frequently open the discussion with the question: "What is this book's central message?"

That is a question readers may be asking after finishing this book. The answer, briefly stated, is (1) that the human mind, unlike the mind of other animals, has intellectual powers; (2) that it is by virtue of these powers that human beings differ radically in kind, not just in degree, from other animals; and (3) that although these intellectual powers cooperate with man's sensitive powers, they differ from the sensitive powers by not being embodied in the brain and sense-organs, but are immaterial powers.

It is the last of these three points that, for many readers, may be most open to doubt. I would therefore like to take this occasion to admit that they have good reason to be in doubt.

In view of the research now going on in the field of artificial intelligence, I am compelled to agree that, sometime in the future, it may be found conclusively that the action of the human brain is not only a necessary condition of our intellectual activity but also its sufficient condition.

If that turns out to be the case, it may dispel all the mysteries about mind except, perhaps, consciousness itself. It is certainly expected to explain, in purely physical or material terms, the human mind's power of conceptual thought and all its other intellectual processes.

The dilemma such doubt requires readers to face is a strong disjunction—an *either/or* with no middle ground. *Either* the intellect is an immaterial power *or* its action, while analytically distinct from that of the brain, is existentially inseparable from it.

Many serious consequences follow from ultimately finding the truth on one or the other side of this dilemma. If, except for the conscious experience that accompanies brain action, all the rest of the mind's activity can be adequately explained in the future by neurophysiology, then man's intellectual power may simply be a higher degree of the intelligence we share with the other animals. We would then also be incorrect in attributing to the human mind two quite different sets of powers: intellectual and sensitive.

I have not yet mentioned in this book what I regard as the most serious consequences of concluding in the future, on the basis of scientific research, that it is a philosophical error to think of the intellect as an immaterial power. Others may not share my view of this matter. They may be irreligious persons who look upon religion as "the poetry in which we believe," to use George Santayana's phrase. They may look upon the stories in the Old and the New Testament as fables, myths of the same kind that are to be found in cultures other than that of the Judeo-Christian West.

To them, it will not come as a shock that denying the immateriality of the intellect deprives two dogmas in Jewish and Christian orthodoxy of any philosophical support. Stated another way, two dogmas of Jewish and Christian faith are called into question by the denial of the intellect's immateriality. One is the immortality of the human soul. The other is the divinity that resides in man, but not in other animals, because human nature has a trace of spirituality in it that explains what is meant by the saying that in man and man alone is to be found the image of God.

Articles of faith are totally beyond proof. A conclusion that can be proved is not and cannot be an article of faith except for those unable to understand the proof. But philosophical arguments and reasoning can be used to make articles of faith intelligible or to lend them rational support that falls short of proof.*

Thus, for example, attempts to prove the existence of God, if successful, do not prove the Jewish or Christian faith in God's existence. A sound philosophical proof of God's existence is at best only a preamble to the Jewish or Christian religious belief in God's existence.†

Philosophical argument is much less adequate with respect to religious faith in immortality than it is with respect to religious faith in God's existence. There is no philosophical argument that proves the immortality of the soul as, in my judgment, there is a sound philosophical argument for the existence of God. But there are sound philosophical arguments for the immateriality of the human intellect. If that conclusion is philosophically true, it at least establishes the possibility, not the actuality, of immortality for human souls.

If, on the contrary, we are in the future compelled to conclude that the human mind is as completely embodied in physical or material organs as are the minds of other animals, then the immortality of the human soul is as impossible

---

*Articles of religious faith cannot be proved, but they are subject to philosophical or scientific disproof. On this point see my book *The Plurality of Religions and the Unity of Truth*, to be published in October 1990.

†See *How to Think About God* (1980), especially Parts I and VI.

as is immortality for the souls of other animals and the souls of plants and vegetables.*

Many readers may attribute a spirituality to human beings that they do not attribute to other animals. They should realize that the only metaphysical significance they can attach to the word "spirituality" is a negative connotation, that of immateriality. If in the future we are compelled to adopt a completely materialistic view of human nature, we should then discard the word "spirituality" from our vocabularies, at least in the metaphysical sense of that word.

If those same readers are also religious Jews or Christians, they should also be shocked to discover that they can no longer proclaim, in the words of Genesis, 1, that man is made in the image of God. For whatever else they may think about God, religious Jews and Christians believe that God is a purely spiritual being. The slender trace of spirituality in man that resides in the immateriality of the human intellect is the only basis for understanding man as made in the image or likeness of God.

Religious Jews and Christians may not then abandon their respective religions, but, in my judgment, the character of those religions will be radically altered. The adoption of a completely materialistic explanation of all natural phenomena, or everything that exists in nature, may not lead to disbelief in God, but it would result in serious changes in the Jewish or Christian beliefs that remain, certainly with respect to man's relation to God and with respect to human destiny, beyond this life and this world.

---

*I am using the word "soul" here in its Aristotelian, not its Platonic, sense— not as signifying a spiritual substance that inhabits the body but as that which, in all living organisms, confers life upon them and all the vital powers they possess. The soul is not in the body as a rower in a rowboat, able to swim away when the rowboat sinks, but rather as form is in matter (i.e., as the die is in the wax).

Experimental induction, 154–55
Experimental psychology, xiii, xv
Extraterrestrial intelligence, 68–75

Faculties, 143–44, 146
Fear, 170
Folly, 181, 182
Fortitude, 169, 172, 186
Free will, xiv, 11, 28, 31, 163–71
 in Roman law, 3
Freud, Sigmund, 183

Galileo, 110
Geach, Peter, 34–35
Generalizations, 34, 36, 58–59, 154–55
General terms, 39
Generic mental powers, 22
Genesis, 4, 192
Geometry, Euclidean, 86
Gifford lectures, 103n, 107n
Gilson, Etienne, 89n
God
 belief in, 191–92
 Cartesian arguments for existence of, 96
 Einstein on, 113
 Hawking on, 107
 love of, 166, 167
 mind of, 91
 as theoretical construct, 119
Goodman, Nelson, 104, 124
Grammar, 128
 universal, 132

Great books seminars, xv, 189
Gregory the Great, St., 185
Grief, 171

Habits, 143–48, 169, 170, 172, 175–76, 179
Hallucinations, 96, 116, 123
Hardy, G. H., 113n
Harvard Univ., viii, 99
Hate, 171
Hawking, Stephen J., 106, 107
Heisenberg, Werner, 105, 107, 108n, 109, 111
Hemispheres of brain, 27
Herbart, Johann, 143
Hierarchical order of grades of life, 71–74
Hobbes, Thomas, 13, 84, 110
Holt, Edwin B., 102
Homo sapiens, 92
How to Read a Book (Adler), xvi
How to Think About God (Adler), 119n
Human nature, 134–39, 148, 149, 159
 spirituality in, 191
Hume, David, 85–86
Hutchins, Robert, 189
"Hymn to Intellectual Beauty" (Shelley), 5

Idealism, 80, 82–86, 88, 96, 101, 126, 139
 absolute, 99
 quantum theory and, 113
 refutations of, 102, 103n